T0025176

PENGUIN SPECIALS

Penguin Specials fill a gap. Written by some of today's most exciting and insightful writers, they are short enough to be read in a single sitting – when you're stuck on a train; in your lunch hour; between dinner and bedtime. Specials can provide a thought-provoking opinion, a primer to bring you up to date, or a striking piece of fiction. They are concise, original and affordable.

To browse digital and print Penguin Specials titles, please refer to **penguin.com.au/penguinspecials**

PENGUIN
SPECIAL

LOWY INSTITUTE

The Lowy Institute is an independent, nonpartisan international policy think tank located in Sydney. It is Australia's leading think tank, providing high-quality research and distinctive perspectives on the issues and trends shaping Australia and the world. The Lowy Institute Papers are peer-reviewed essays and research papers on key international issues.

Sir Lawrence Freedman is Emeritus Professor
of War Studies at King's College London and
a Nonresident Fellow of the Lowy Institute.
Among his books are *Strategy: A History* (2013)
and *Command: The Politics of Military Operations
from Korea to Ukraine* (2022).

LOWY INSTITUTE

Modern Warfare: Lessons from Ukraine

A LOWY INSTITUTE PAPER

LAWRENCE FREEDMAN

PENGUIN BOOKS

UK | USA | Canada | Ireland | Australia
India | New Zealand | South Africa | China

Penguin Books is part of the Penguin Random House group of companies
whose addresses can be found at global.penguinrandomhouse.com.

First published by Penguin Books, 2023

Copyright © Lowy Institute for International Policy, 2023

The moral right of the author has been asserted.

All rights reserved. No part of this publication may be reproduced,
published, performed in public or communicated to the public in any
form or by any means without prior written permission from
Penguin Random House Australia Pty Ltd or its authorised licensees.

Cover image by Sergey Bobok/AFP via Getty Images
Typeset by Midland Typesetters, Australia

Printed and bound in Australia by Griffin Press, an accredited
ISO AS/NZS 14001 Environmental Management Systems printer

A catalogue record for this
book is available from the
National Library of Australia

ISBN 978 1 76134 305 6

penguin.com.au

MIX
Paper | Supporting
responsible forestry
FSC® C018684

CONTENTS

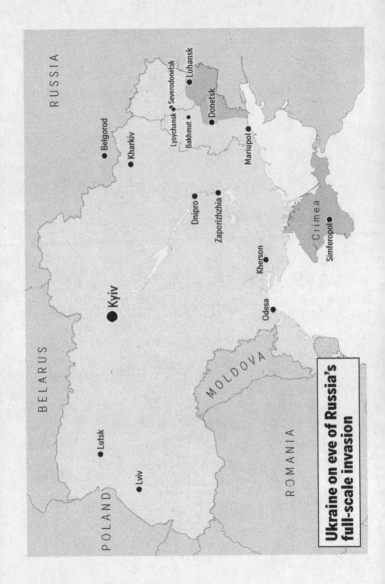

Ukraine on eve of Russia's full-scale invasion

Introduction

Russia's war on Ukraine began in March 2014 when Crimea was seized and annexed. This was followed by violence in eastern Ukraine involving Russian-sponsored militias and eventually the regular Russian army, as the militias were unable to cope with the Ukrainian army. The violence never quite went away. Agreements were reached at Minsk in Belarus in September 2014 and February 2015 on ceasefires and peace settlements, but they were never fully implemented.

Then came the invasion of Ukraine on 24 February 2022, leading to intense fighting between two substantial industrial states. This fighting is a great human tragedy and has triggered a major international crisis. At the same time, it is also viewed as a learning opportunity for other armed forces.

It illustrates in vivid and often distressing ways the lethality of modern weapons and the variety of operations they can support through the seasons of the year in a large country with varying terrain. It has shown how whole populations can suddenly face desperate situations that they must either flee or endure.

It is always dangerous to generalise from specific cases. The unique circumstances of this war are unlikely to be replicated. The conditions would be quite different in future Middle Eastern or Indo-Pacific wars. In the latter case, maritime considerations would be to the fore. Moreover, this war has been through its own transformations. Conclusions drawn from its early stages already look questionable. Yet it is also important to reflect on what we have seen. In this short book, my reflections, inevitably preliminary because the war is not yet over and there is much more to learn about its conduct, concentrate on strategic choices. I consider the factors that influenced those making the key political and military decisions on war aims and the use of available capabilities to meet them. Both sides have fought using their own theories of war.

I describe these distinctive approaches as 'classical' for the Ukrainians, in which they try to confine the fighting to battles, and 'total' for the Russians, in that in addition to the battles, they are prepared to target civil society. The war provides an opportunity to compare these two approaches, both in terms of the realism of their assumptions and their effectiveness. This is not a full history of the war and there are certain aspects, such as maritime operations, that are not covered. My focus is on routes to victory – one that concentrates on control of territory and the other that adds coercive attacks on civil society.

My sympathies in this war are entirely with Ukraine. Russian President Vladimir Putin's rationale for war was flimsy and fabricated. Russia was the aggressor, and it has behaved cruelly and criminally. Right, however, does not always triumph in war. Might usually makes the difference. The fact that Ukrainian forces have been able to defeat much more substantial Russian forces in some important battles does not ensure eventual victory, but it does highlight the importance of strategic choices and distinctive ideas about the conduct of war.

At first, many governments and pundits assumed that Russia would win the conventional stage of this war without too much difficulty. Problems were considered more likely to develop as it became necessary to pacify a hostile population and deal with an insurgency. In the event, the Russian army failed in its most important early battle, to take the Ukrainian capital, Kyiv, and within weeks had to retreat, concentrating thereafter on seeking to hold territory seized in the south and east of Ukraine early in the war, and taking more territory to align the occupation with President Putin's objectives (which have varied in ambition during the course of the war). Ukraine's objective, from which it has not deviated, is to push the Russians out.

This has resulted in a series of battles of great intensity, with much of the fighting in urban areas and leading to high casualties. There are no recent precedents that could provide guidance on how this war would be conducted. Analyses of conflicts involving one or more of the major military powers are of little value. Some of those conflicts were limited and scrappy; others were deadly and significant. All, however, were asymmetrical, in that they were fought between entities with quite different capabilities, especially when it came to air power. Western armies defeated much weaker opponents in the conventional stages of their Middle Eastern wars before getting bogged down in insurgencies, which might have provided some warning to Russia. Russia also defeated weaker opponents – in Chechnya, Georgia, Crimea and eastern Ukraine, and then in support of the Syrian government – but none of these operations came close to the sort of major war for which the great powers continued to prepare. Prior to Ukraine, the most recent example of a conventional war with relatively modern equipment was the short Armenia-Azerbaijan conflict of September 2020.

The scale and ferocity of the Russo-Ukrainian war is unique in recent times in providing insights into the possible character of a great power war. This is why it is already being examined for what it reveals about issues such as whether defence remains the strongest form of warfare, the importance of combined arms, the demands of logistics, and the challenges of command, as well as the roles of individual weapons systems, from tanks to drones. There have been opportunities to assess how advanced military systems and innovative tactics perform in combat as commanders on both sides have had to search for solutions to novel military problems.

At the time of writing (early August 2023), the Russo-Ukrainian war has been going for a year and a half. Whatever the skill with which past operations have been planned and executed, what matters is the situation when (and if) a ceasefire comes, whether a win for one side or some sort of draw. That will depend not only on how coming battles are fought, but also the ability of both sides to keep their armies supplied with troops, equipment, and ammunition, and how well their societies and economies cope with the stresses and strains of war. This in turn may depend on the quality of their international support.

The rush to draw lessons must therefore be tempered by an appreciation of the wider context in which this war has taken place. Wars are not set up as deep educational experiences. They do not follow standard patterns, and each one has unique features that mean what happens in one may not be the best guide to what might happen in the next. The best lessons to be drawn tend to be about the inevitable pitfalls that accompany any military operation – the danger of neglecting logistics, and the folly of underestimating opponents.

Another reason for caution is that the elements of symmetry and asymmetry in the respective force structures, and therefore the nature of their inter-actions, have changed over the course of the conflict. When it began, Russia had the advantage in most departments but as it was unable to make them count, its advantages began to slip away. As it used up its best equipment and took casualties among its most experienced troops, it struggled to find adequate replacements. This meant that its weapons systems became older, and its troops greener. Until mass mobilisation was ordered in late September 2022, personnel shortages grew in severity. With

Russian air power having less impact than antici-pated, advances have depended largely on artillery barrages and costly infantry assaults backed by armoured vehicles. By contrast, over time, Ukraine has received more advanced systems from the West, at first largely for defence, but then to support more offensive operations, although it has lost many of its most experienced troops.

But it is the strategic asymmetry that has been most marked. Each side is fighting in quite dis-tinctive ways, reflecting their circumstances – one is invading and the other defending – and national predispositions, influenced on the Ukrainian side by its Western partners and on the Russian side by the weight of history and its other recent wars. Because the war is being fought on Ukrainian territory, Ukrainian forces have every incentive to avoid harm-ing civilians. Russia, by contrast, has made no effort to spare civilians and has deliberately targeted the critical infrastructure necessary to keep Ukraine's economy and society functioning.

This war also allows us to explore the meaning of warfare in the digital age. New information tech-nologies have transformed the practice of warfare by improving the efficiency with which the traditional instruments of war can be used. They also open pos-sibilities for new forms of warfare, such as targeted information campaigns and attacks against the networks upon which states depend, not only to conduct military operations, but for the effective functioning of the economy and society.

CHAPTER I

Warfare:
classical and total

CLASSICAL WAR

The classical way of warfare, which dominated Western military thought prior to the First World War, was all about battles. Michael Howard identifies the classical school of military theorists as those who 'sought in the chaos of war for clear, consistent, interdependent principles as a guide to understanding and action'. He identifies the British writer Henry Lloyd as showing the way in the eighteenth century, with Antoine Henri Jomini and Carl von Clausewitz the prime exponents during the nineteenth, drawing on their experience of the Napoleonic Wars. This led to a sharp focus on decisive battle and the elimination of the enemy army.[1] Strategy was about getting an army in a position to fight a battle; tactics was about the fighting.

Victory was decided by whichever army occupied the battlefield, the number of enemy soldiers killed or captured, and equipment destroyed. In this way, battles determined the outcome of wars. This classical approach was bolstered by a normative framework that covered the treatment of prisoners and non-combatants, and assumed that the defeated enemy would accept the verdict of battle.

This reflects an ideal type. These are not so much descriptions but useful simplifications – constructs that pick up on the essential characteristics of a particular phenomenon to help show it in its purest form to facilitate analysis and guide action. Though these ideal types may shape strategy, actual practice will differ because of the nature of the adversary's strategy, the operational conditions, and the wider political context. As an ideal type, classical war would be conducted separately from civil society and be decided through battle, with the belligerents gaining advantage through the speed of their decision-making, the quality of their technology, and the professionalism of their tactics. The approach continues to influence Western military thinking. Those working with this framework have been particularly enamoured with operational concepts based on out-manoeuvring the enemy in battle and avoiding trading firepower in attritional warfare, and so tending towards a true ideal in which all casualties, military as well as civilian, can be reduced.

Despite the normative requirement to reduce and, if possible, remove the risks of causing harm to non-combatants, this could only be achieved in very remote areas. Moreover, to the extent that wars are about sovereignty over defined areas of territory – and mostly they are – then populations matter, whether they are to be protected, won over, pushed out, or repressed. There is therefore a cruel logic to war that makes it difficult to confine its effects to battles. On one view, prevalent in the West, the implications for military strategy need not be large. The military still has a professional duty, enshrined in the Geneva Conventions, to use force in a proportionate manner and only risk civilian casualties on grounds of military necessity.

In US military discourse in the 1980s, theorists lamented a decline in the art of generalship and over-reliance on firepower. Instead of preparing for intensive artillery exchanges, they wanted to encourage imaginative and decisive operations that could bring wars to an end quickly at low cost. They had in mind German-type blitzkriegs, which used speed to bypass the enemy's strongest positions and catch them by surprise. With new technologies, the possibilities for such operations appeared to grow. After the Iraqi army was roundly defeated in February 1991, enthusiastic theorists started to describe forms of warfare based on exceptional situational awareness combined with precision weapons, fired from a distance, and marked by swift, audacious moves that would leave the enemy discombobulated and in disarray.

A classical military victory against a palpably inferior adversary might be achieved quickly, assuming the enemy plays by the same rules. But against another serious military power, the path to victory might be less clear. Offensives that fail to overcome entrenched defences can lead to long and gruelling wars. Effective offensives require punching holes in the defence using superior firepower or surprising the enemy by advancing in unexpected ways and manoeuvring around established positions. Success will be marked by the enemy's rapid retreat, or encirclement, until a point is reached where the enemy is unable to recover. That is the aim: defeat the enemy's armed forces decisively to create the conditions for a favourable political settlement.

To maximise the possibility of victory, especially against a potentially strong adversary, wars are best started with the maximum of surprise. There are a variety of ways to achieve surprise – preparations not detected, intentions not discerned, capabilities not appreciated, timing not anticipated, direction not expected, or some permutation of these factors. Whatever the source of the surprise, the first blows must be made to count. An element of surprise, whether in direction, weight, or timing, has led in the past to decisive victories. During the first year of the Second World War, Germany achieved apparently decisive military victories that took individual countries out of the war, at least temporarily. In the end, they turned out not to be conclusive because the British were not defeated and continued to fight.

In June 1941, Germany invaded the Soviet Union. In December 1941, Japan attacked the US naval base at Pearl Harbor. In both cases, the aim was to gain a vital advantage against an adversary with whom they assumed war to be inevitable. Their attacks were bold in execution and complete in surprise. They were also reckless in taking on much larger powers before existing enemies had been defeated (the British in Germany's case and China in Japan's case). Both gambles failed. At first, it looked like the Soviet Union might be defeated, but it held on and gradually the size of the country, its harsh climate, reserves of strength, and Nazi mistakes turned the tide of war. There was never much chance that the United States would be defeated by Japan once the Americans mobilised. The war ended with the occupation of Japan.

A classical victory depends on an enemy clearly defeated or at least left with no chance of recovering its position in future battles. Even if caught out, badly hurt, and perhaps conceding some territory, a defender that still has functioning forces can slow down the attacker, gaining time to regroup and reconstitute its forces, and perhaps bringing in allies. Time gained by the defender can therefore be used to mobilise reserves, develop counter-offensives, and attract significant international backing. And then, even if the defending forces are defeated, there will be a further challenge in subjugating the country. Can a new government sympathetic to the attacker be installed? What are the possibilities of partisan warfare, of sabotage and ambushes so that occupations become costly and frustrating?

The classical approach assumed that a decisive military victory would almost automatically lead to a political victory. The defeated party would need to accept that territory taken was probably lost forever. Yet in practice, wars drag on. The loser in battle might accept the temporary loss of territory without making a permanent concession. There might be a ceasefire but not a peace settlement. The struggle might continue in occupied territory through irregular warfare. The victory might simply be incomplete, so that the war becomes a test of endurance, with both sides having to mobilise people and resources to continue the fight, step up production of armaments and ammunition, perhaps with the help of a willing external supplier, and put the whole society and economy on a war footing. These were the reasons why, however easy it might be to start wars, they were often difficult to stop.

The problem with the classical approach, therefore, is that whatever the intent, wars become more demanding of the wider society the longer they drag on. This puts a premium on making the first blows count, but even with surprise and maximum effort, the first blows might not achieve enough, especially against an opponent with reserves of strength. There could be arguments in favour of initiating a war with a surprise attack even without confidence that this could conclude hostilities quickly, especially if it was assumed that a war was inevitable. In such circumstances, it might still be best to take the initiative and gain whatever advantage possible before the prolonged struggle to come. This was the Japanese rationale in 1941. There are also examples of quick victories resulting from surprise attacks, as with Israel's demolition of Egypt's air force on 5 June 1967 (although this war also eventually demonstrated how conquering and occupying another's territory could lead to persistent terrorism and insurgency). Examples of surprise attacks that failed to deliver quick victories include North Korea's move against the South in June 1950, and Iraq's against Iran three decades later. These failed for two different reasons – the first because an international coalition led by the United States came to the aid of South Korea before it was completely overrun, and the second because Iraq lacked the strength to overwhelm Iran and soon had to cope with Iran's counter-attack, leading to a war that continued until 1988.

Any war affects the people and places where it is being fought, even if this is the result of carelessness and indifference more than malign intent. Civilians flee from areas where fighting is taking place or are caught in villages, towns, and cities in contention. In urban warfare, regular forces will feel they have little choice but to occupy buildings that are either residential or used for civilian purposes (such as schools and hospitals) as cover to fire at the enemy, so inviting return fire. In addition, the infrastructure required to support military operations can also support the civilian. Transport, communications, and energy networks tend to be dual purpose. They will be attacked to disrupt the enemy's military effort even though that will also disrupt civilian life.

When facing an insurgency, restraint makes sense if host populations are to be kept loyal and supportive, yet is still a challenge when the enemy takes sanctuary in civilian areas, merging with the local population until they come out as terrorists, guerrillas, and militias. Even when engaged in regular operations, precision requires not only accurate weapons but also reliable intelligence, so that enemies can be identified and targeted with confidence. When troops are engaged in counter-insurgency operations, enemy militants can seem indistinguishable from civilians, and acting with restraint because of the danger to civilians can be high risk, especially when there are well-grounded suspicions that civilians are sympathetic to the enemy. Considerations of force protection tend to take precedence over civilian casualty avoidance.

A classical approach to warfare concentrates on defeating the enemy's forces. When this is done, victory should be declared. But the more this effort is thwarted, the more it depends on the wider society and the more attritional it becomes. All war, therefore, tends to blur civil-military distinctions and increasingly puts civilians at risk. Over time, there can be a shift from fighting the enemy's forces to fighting the whole society. It is, nonetheless, still important to distinguish between strategies that prioritise defeating the enemy's armed forces and those that seek a route to victory by affecting the will of the enemy to continue with the war by deliberate attacks on social and economic structures.

TOTAL WAR

The total war approach, once widespread in the West and still evident in Moscow, accepts that armed forces do not only fight each other. They can also be used for coercive and repressive purposes. In addition to encounters along classical lines, in a total war there will be further layers of violence involving attacks on the economic and social systems supporting the enemy's war effort, including the civilian population. Such an approach makes assumptions about the fragility of the enemy's socio-political system and its resilience. The total war approach supplements rather than replaces a classical approach. It normally becomes more important if a classical approach has failed to secure the enemy's capitulation and an element of coercion must be added. It cannot be conducted entirely separate from classical war: enemy territory might need to be taken or air defences overcome.

The origins of the total approach can be traced back to the First World War when the limits of the classical approach were exposed. The Germans began the war with an ambitious offensive designed to defeat France quickly. Instead, they got caught up in a long and gruelling slog in which they struggled to cope with the superior economic and demographic strengths of their enemies. After the war, there was still interest in how a victory might be achieved along classical lines, for example by using tanks to revive the possibility of rapid offensives. But the arduous experience of that war encouraged a search for alternative paths to victory.

Air power seemed to offer an easy answer. Aircraft could fly over the trenches and reach the heart of the enemy. Instead of concentrating on troops ready for the fight and under military discipline, helpless civilians could be attacked, likely triggering panic. Instead of forcing the enemy government to capitulate because of the annihilation of their army or the occupation of their land, it could be compelled to surrender because their population was desperate, hit by a succession of massive air raids that showered them with high explosives, incendiaries, or even poison gas. The use of air power to achieve a decisive victory in this way was described as 'strategic', while use in support of classical military operations was merely 'tactical'. (This distinction was carried forward into the nuclear age.)

There was no difficulty finding a rationale to explain why civilians should be attacked. Armies drew on civilian infrastructure to fight. The munitions factories depended on their workforce. When more troops were needed, civilians were drafted. There were no innocents when the whole country was on a war footing. Moreover, the governments that decided on war and peace depended on popular support, especially in democracies. That meant the electors could not escape the consequences of their choices. Furthermore, vulnerable civilians, suffering under incessant attacks from the air, might be turned against the war. During the inter-war years, it came to be assumed that future wars would be total and that they would open with massive, and potentially decisive, air raids.

Despite initial caution, restraints on the use of force against civilians were progressively abandoned during the Second World War, leading to immense suffering. The bombs could not be aimed accurately. Targets were easier to spot during daylight raids, but that meant aircrews were more vulnerable. At night, it was hard to pick out discrete facilities, but cities could still be attacked, as was demonstrated in the Blitz on London and later the huge air raids against Germany and Japan. This total war logic culminated in the use of two atomic bombs in August 1945, which seemed to confirm their strategic quality because Japan soon surrendered.

Not only the means of war but also the ends had become more total. War was about much more than who owned some disputed territory, and now included the objectionable ethnicity, religion, and ideology of the enemy people. The fact that the enemy society had the nerve to resist encouraged demonisation. In these ways, the suppression or even elimination of whole groups could become a distinctive war aim. Civilians died not only because they were unfortunate enough to be close to a battle or some vital facility, doing important war work, or even because lowering their morale might create pressure on their leaders, but because of who they were. In such cases, harming civilians was not just a route to victory but the purpose of victory.

The influence of a total war philosophy on the Nazis and their conduct during the war, including in territories they occupied, encouraged the view that a total war was extreme in its methods and absolute in its aims. In practice, this was always a matter of degree, although the Nazis pushed the limits as far as they could go. For my purposes, a total war approach simply refers to a readiness to attack deliberately and methodically the enemy's socio-economic system as a route to victory.

What in the classical model appeared to be the result of carelessness and uncertainty appeared desirable in the total model. There was no need to worry about directing firepower – artillery, rockets, missiles, aircraft – away from civilian targets. Precision became less important or, if embraced, could facilitate attacks on particularly significant targets, such as refineries, power stations, railway hubs, government buildings, hospitals, and schools.

The legal position against total war hardened after 1945, with a raft of amendments to the Geneva Conventions designed to protect civilians. The 1951 Genocide Convention prohibited attempts to eliminate or erase the identity of whole communities. This meant that embracing a total war model essentially amounted to being ready to commit war crimes, although of course those prepared to commit such crimes either do not recognise the legal framework or else they believe that the victims have been disqualified from its protections because of their inherent characteristics or their own, even greater, crimes.

As serious a problem with total war was the lack of strategic validation. If there was a purpose to attacking civil society, it was to influence enemy decision-makers to look for ways out of the war. As with any coercive effort, it could not dictate the target's reaction. Compliance was one possibility; angry resistance was another. To work as a stand-alone strategy however, total war required that the victim population was unable to adapt to the terror and hardship of their situation and also that there were political processes that could turn their misery into a demand for a change in the government's strategy. It was not enough that the people were miserable. They must act on their misery. Given that it was not their government making their life miserable (other than by refusing to capitulate), then it was likely and in fact quite usual that the greatest anger would be directed at the perpetrator of the crimes.

As Second World War air raids demonstrated, the resilience of ordinary people and of modern societies had been underestimated. If anything, the raids increased dependence on the state and national solidarity. Only with the war's finale and the atom bombs dropped on Hiroshima and Nagasaki was the deadly promise of air power realised. Previous air raids had killed as many, but this time, the devastation required only single weapons. Their impact was emphasised by the surrender of an already beleaguered Japan. Even without the bomb, however, Japan would likely have struggled to keep the war going for much longer.

Modern warfare is therefore layered. At the start of a war, operations may take a classical form as the initiating state seeks an early defeat of its adversary.

If it fails, and the longer the war goes on, the more likely it is that civilian assets and infrastructure will be attacked and degraded, whether because of the intensity of the battles, efforts to interfere with supply lines and defence production, or as a deliberate attempt to raise the stakes. As these attacks move from affecting support for front-line military operations, they become more coercive. Coercive strategies are inherently less reliable than the classical military operations that promise, if they succeed, direct control over enemy territory. That is why wars tend to start with a clash of regular forces. The methods of total war are often the result of frustration, an inability to find another way of hurting a resisting enemy, or a stalemate in classical warfare. On their own, it is difficult for total war strategies to succeed, as they still require armies to follow through to seize control of disputed territory or, in the event of surrender, take over the enemy's capital. At issue is whether they add value or detract because of the resources that must be expended to make them work.

THE NUCLEAR AND DIGITAL REVOLUTIONS

Even though the August 1945 atomic bombings came at the end of a long and brutal war that had spread across the world, and seen numerous new developments in weapons and tactics, this was recognised at once to be a transformational moment. It was the logical conclusion of all those tendencies towards total war, including the use of dirigibles, aircraft, and missiles to attack centres of population, their deadly zenith apparently reached with the fire-bombing of Tokyo in March 1945. But the scale and immediacy of the destruction caused by single weapons, coupled with the insidious and lingering presence of radiation, plus the subsequent Japanese surrender, meant that the role of mass destruction in war moved to a new level.

When yet another level was reached in the early 1950s with the arrival of thermonuclear weapons, with no evident limits on their explosive yield and with the Soviet Union acquiring the same capabilities as the United States, there were profound implications for the readiness of states to resort to war. This led to the generation of a new strategic concept geared towards managing crises and retaining some sort of equilibrium in great power relations. The possibility of a surprise attack (a 'first strike') was seen to be key. It would appear too dangerous to contemplate, so long as the other side was sure in its ability to retaliate (a 'second strike'). This led to what came to be described as a condition of 'mutual assured destruction'. Total war no longer seemed an option for the great powers because it implied collective suicide. Despite the deep antagonism of the Cold War and the acquisition of massive nuclear arsenals by both the United States and the Soviet Union, mutual deterrence took hold, and a catastrophic Third World War was avoided.

The nuclear revolution was not the only technology-driven transformation in the practice of warfare. The changes associated with the digital age were both more incremental and far-reaching. The microchip was invented in the 1950s and the circuits printed upon them became ever more complex, even as the chips became tinier. Computers have moved from performing basic calculations faster than humans to out-thinking humans in a whole range of areas, with the promise of more to come as artificial intelligence advances. Their influence has affected the acquisition, assessment, and dissemination of intelligence, navigation, and communications, the precision and range of weapons, and the speed of military decision-making and command networks. All standard military tasks have become more efficient.

But whereas the impact of nuclear energy was stark and unmistakeable, promising an absolute catastrophe if unleashed and so providing a compelling reason for restraint, no generally agreed framework emerged to describe and evaluate the impact of the digital age, perhaps because its influence was incremental and ubiquitous. One reason for this was that digitisation, with its fast networks and ease of communication, promised greater efficiency in all human affairs. This created new dependencies and vulnerabilities. Bad actors, from criminals to hostile states, saw opportunities to disrupt and manipulate. This opened up possibilities for hostile action away from the battlefield, with cyberattacks targeting societies directly rather than first having to defeat their armed forces. Another complication was that digital age systems did not replace all that went before. They worked with the systems of the industrial age, the platforms for carrying weapons and moving them to places where they could be fired to the greatest effect, such as artillery and tanks, aircraft and warships. Digital age systems did not so much replace those of the industrial age as render them more effective.

'Smart' munitions first made their appearance in the early 1970s. By the time of the 1991 Gulf War, the quality of sensors, data processing, and networks could be appreciated. The battlefield (now 'battlespace') became far more transparent and decision-making far more rapid, exposing ever more targets to attack as soon as they could be spotted and tracked. This encouraged talk of a Revolution in

Military Affairs (RMA). Fitting in with concepts of manoeuvre warfare, RMA offered a model that was dispassionate, influenced neither by desperation nor vengeance, marked by careful calculations of risks and options, not only more precise but also more civilised.

Any optimism on this score was soon dashed by the attacks against New York's World Trade Center and the Pentagon on 11 September 2001. Instead of preparing for a high-technology, high-intensity war against a 'peer competitor', the priority became a much lower-intensity fight against ruthless terrorists. Then the big counter-insurgency campaigns in Iraq and Afghanistan drew attention to challenges quite different to those faced in conventional warfare against regular armies, requiring a sophisticated understanding of local politics and culture, more so than demonstrated by the Western powers. Instead of wars conducted away from civil society, these were wars 'among the people', to use General Rupert Smith's phrase.[2]

Meanwhile, it seemed unlikely that the systems associated with the RMA would ever be fully tested in a major war between symmetrically armed industrial powers, largely because of the continuing fear of nuclear war. This century has seen revived talk of great power competition and tensions, yet still a consensus, developed during the Cold War, that the fear of a nuclear confrontation would act as a formidable restraint, preventing escalation into an all-out hot war. The strategic implications of the new capabilities changed with the move away from big wars between great powers towards expeditionary interventions in civil conflicts, guerrilla warfare, and terrorism. Western commanders would no doubt seek to employ their forces with precision and keep casualties to a minimum, but opponents might not fight in the same way.

THE GREY AREA

The biggest claim, made with increased frequency from the early 1990s, was that 'cyberwar is coming'.[3] The argument that networked societies could be brought to a juddering halt by well-timed and targeted hacking gained traction over subsequent decades because of the range and frequency of cyber-attacks, although many of these were more criminal than political. With regard to future war, a variety of activities could be covered under this 'cyber' heading. They largely corresponded to familiar 'behind the front lines' activities – sabotage, propaganda, subversion, and espionage. As commonly discussed in the West, cyberattacks were closest to sabotage – interfering with administrative networks or power supplies – and propaganda – using social media to spread fake news and false narratives.

Views on what these activities might achieve were influenced by Russian actions beginning in 2014. Russia's cyber operations were linked with its total war perspective because of the assumption that all socio-political systems, including their own, were fragile and could be subverted. Moscow was both convinced that Western governments were stirring up disaffected Russians and also that it could undermine these same governments by spreading alarm and despondency among their populations. Non-traditional forms of warfare seemed to appeal to Russia because of its interest in finding ways of hurting others while still claiming innocence and avoiding direct confrontation with the West. In 2014, Moscow brought a wide range of capabilities together – from regular forces and sponsored militias to cyberhackers and social media propagandists. This approach was described as 'hybrid'. When this term was first introduced in 2006, with Israel's fight against Hezbollah in Lebanon in mind, it was the combination of regular and irregular that was highlighted. By 2014, it seemed as if the Russian leadership had developed a whole new theory of conflict around mixing and matching different capabilities. Although this claim was exaggerated, Russia was actively exploring the possibilities of attacks against digital networks. One question was whether these activities, as modern forms of sabotage, subversion, and propaganda, were seen as supplements to direct military action or sources of a decisive advantage on their own. Their potential might appeal to those working in a tradition, going back to Soviet times, that assumed the fragility of opposing political systems.

Thereafter, at least prior to 2022, it was often argued that it suited Russia better to work in this murky 'grey zone', avoiding both the risks of war and the rules of peace. This concern about a grey zone extended to Iran and China. The point was not that the activities undertaken in this zone were non-violent, as in many cases they clearly were not. What was significant about them was that they could be undertaken covertly, or at least with some level of deniability, and, most importantly, that they could be sustained, possibly indefinitely, without spilling over into an open conflict that might escalate into all-out war. At times, they were hyped up as if they could be equivalent to war, able to achieve decisive strategic results on their own. In practice, they became part of the mix, adding an extra layer to conflict, influencing both the classical and total war approaches. They could be considered in terms of total war not because of the scale of destruction implied but because they posed threats to a nation's whole socio-economic structure in addition to its military power.

This grey area was a feature of the renewed great power competition, appearing as a means of undermining adversaries while avoiding all-out war and keeping the risks of escalation under control. Away from great power conflict, it was not so important to stay below the threshold. This meant that armed conflict was most likely to occur between or with weaker powers, unsupported by stronger powers, precisely because of the fear of escalation.

CLASSICAL UKRAINE VERSUS TOTAL RUSSIA

Western countries continue to embrace classical approaches to war in principle because they fit with traditional 'just war' thinking, allowing for the use of armed force only to right a grievous wrong and, so long as it can be conducted in a proportionate manner, with the minimum of harm to non-combatants. As important, it also fits with technological trends, which allow force to be applied with ever greater precision and discrimination. Under the influence of the RMA, Western militaries increasingly viewed civilian deaths as evidence of political and operational failure. Their frustration was that while they had developed the weapons and concepts for warfare to take full advantage of the digital age, they became caught up in counter-terrorist and counter-insurgency campaigns in which it was a constant struggle to separate enemy fighters from ordinary civilians, and in which the campaigns were decided by factors such as governance, economic reform, and social justice, well outside the military domain. Even battles to liberate cities from unpopular occupiers – such as supporting Iraqi government forces in the 2016–17 operation to push Islamic State out of Mosul – could lead to devastating effects on civilians.

Russia has never fully disavowed the total war model. In the wars against Chechnya to prevent secession, tactics were often quite brutal, and the capital Grozny was left flattened. In operations to support the Syrian government against rebels from 2015 onwards, Russia not only provided diplomatic cover for Syrian use of chemical weapons and 'barrel bombs', but also used air power to make life as difficult as possible for civilians. This was the other side of the coin to precision guidance – the same systems used to avoid hitting civilians could also be used to target them. In Aleppo, for example, Russian aircraft deliberately struck hospitals, often using coordinates handed to them by the United Nations to help Russia avoid these buildings.

The Russian approach was insensitive to civilian (or for that matter, military) casualties and ruthless in its determination to defeat its opponents. In its narratives surrounding military operations, Russia sought to demonstrate that the victims deserved all they got, and that Russia was only responding to severe provocation. Putin is widely blamed for a 'false flag' operation in August 1999 involving apparent terrorist attacks against residential accommodation to provide a pretext for the second Chechen War, which he launched immediately after.

Putin's strategies, including in Ukraine in 2014, were apparently indifferent to humanitarian costs, but Putin also sought to limit his liabilities. The Syrian Civil War was the deadliest the region has known, but Russia confined itself to air power, so it was not caught up in any heavy fighting. The 2014 annexation of Crimea involved little fighting. In the Donbas, Russia sponsored separatist groups, often led by Russians, to undertake a rebellion against a new government in Kyiv.

Russia's wars, other than Syria, were conducted on territory that was either part of the Russian Federation, as with Chechnya, or in territory that was part of the former Soviet Union, which Moscow did not view as truly 'foreign', not least because of the presence of large numbers of Russian speakers, as with Ukraine and Georgia. Yet in none of these conflicts was avoidance of harm to civilians a priority. In both Chechnya and Syria, Russian tactics were unsparing, relying on brute force to overwhelm their enemies. This was also the case in Ukraine in 2022, except here the enemy was not a rebel militia but an increasingly well-organised and professional army. Because of the resistance faced, Russia resorted to attacks on civil society, while Ukrainian forces, largely because they were fighting on their own land and were employing Western systems, followed a classical approach. The contrast between the two approaches has become sharper during the war.

The Russian approach to Ukraine was total in objectives – the aim initially was regime change ('denazification' and 'demilitarisation'). After the failure of the early attack on Kyiv, it focused on partition, and in September 2022, the amount of Ukrainian territory sought expanded from Donetsk and Luhansk to include the oblasts of Kherson and Zaporizhzhia. Yet these ambitious objectives were not combined with a whole-hearted commitment to do whatever was necessary to meet them. President Putin spoke of a 'special military operation' as if it was limited action, short of full-scale war. It was more than six months into the war before

Russia was put onto a war footing, with defence production prioritised and large numbers of troops mobilised.

In an article in *Foreign Affairs*, Andrei Soldatov and Irina Borogan describe this war as 'not quite total', as 'halfway to hell'.[4] They contrast the maximalist course set by Putin (subjugating all of Ukraine) with the measures adopted. Not enough troops were committed at the start, and the September mobilisation was partial rather than total. There were hints about using nuclear weapons, although these always remained ambiguous. The domestic measures promised (or threatened) to protect the economy or clamp down on dissent were not fully implemented. Soldatov and Borogan argued that this had advantages for Putin:

> By staking out a maximalist stance on the war, the Kremlin can suggest to the West that it is prepared to do whatever it takes to win in Ukraine, without necessarily having to make good on its threats. At home, meanwhile, the Russian government can convey to ordinary Russians that it has the option of tightening the screws further, but that it is not going out of its way to alienate the population. In both cases, the strategy offers Putin an open path toward further escalation, but without the immediate costs.

Conceptually, as already noted, to say that a war is total does not mean that it has moved to the extremity, only that it engages with the whole of society. Soldatov's and Borogan's analysis was more about how Putin was keeping options open. It raised the question of whether it would ever be possible to achieve maximum objectives without a whole-hearted commitment. Yet the limits Russia placed on the conduct of the war have been progressively eased. From early on, Ukrainian civil society was under attack, with no target evidently off limits. This is the distinguishing feature of a total war approach.

The most important limitation was the non-use of nuclear weapons, the ultimate symbols of total war. There were regular expressions of concern that Russia might use them, especially if facing a battlefield defeat. In practice, nuclear weapons played a critical role from the start, as deterrents, setting the boundaries to the conflict. Putin invoked the nuclear threat when announcing the war to warn North Atlantic Treaty Organization (NATO) countries against direct intervention. At the same time, his desire to avoid a war with the alliance deterred him from using nuclear weapons within Ukraine and also from ordering attacks on neighbouring NATO countries.

Unlike Russia, Ukraine did not have a nuclear arsenal – it gave up the arsenal it had inherited from the Soviet Union in 1994. And unlike Russia, it did not deploy its armed forces beyond its borders in support of clients and allies, other than in peace-keeping operations. The Ukrainian armed forces had the same Soviet and Warsaw Pact roots, which were reflected in much of the equipment with which they started the war, and might have been expected to be reflected in much of their command structure and operational concepts. The Soviet influence was still present in Ukraine among older commanders and in the respect for hierarchy. After 2014, however, Ukrainian forces came under the influence of Western military thinking. Under Zelensky, new senior commanders were brought in to provide more dynamic leadership. A known reformer, General Valery Zaluzhny, became Commander-in-Chief of the Armed Forces in July 2021. During the course of the war, these new commanders have fought with NATO support and, increasingly, weaponry and concepts.

Contrasting objectives required different strategies. Russia was seeking to overthrow a government and occupy a country, while Ukraine was defending its territory and seeking to liberate what had been occupied. Ukraine had every incentive to spare civilian suffering. Given the claims made in Moscow about Ukraine really being part of Russia – so that the invasion was a form of liberation – and the cross-border ties of family and language, one might have expected Russia to also avoid harm to civilians. Instead, civil society was attacked from the start of the war. If the aim was to cause harm to Ukraine, Russia's campaign has been a tragic success, with a quarter of the population (ten million) displaced, of which more than six million left the country. Life in occupied territories was reshaped to turn it into an extension of Russia. In those areas under Russian occupation, there have been measures designed to impose 'Russification' (for example with language, education, and currency) while using torture and executions to inhibit resistance. This has occurred alongside the war crimes, from looting to sexual abuse, that stem from general indiscipline. In addition, and reinforcing the contrast in approaches, Russia has mounted deliberate strikes with coercive intent on civilian infrastructure, and also hit apartment buildings, hospitals, and schools, with the intention of undermining support for the Ukrainian government and perhaps punishing the Ukrainians for their opposition to the invasion.

Another example of the deterrent effect of nuclear weapons was Washington's deliberate restriction of Ukraine's ability to attack Russian territory, at least in ways in which the United States might be implicated. Until well into the war, Ukraine was denied the long-range rocket artillery and aircraft that would allow them to strike deeper and more often. The result was that Russia fought a total war on Ukrainian territory without facing a serious risk of anything equivalent. Over time, the Ukrainians developed more means for mounting attacks on targets in Russia using drones and sabotage. Initially, these were relatively few and not at scale, but their numbers and impact grew. They became a means of demonstrating to Moscow that it could not defend its own territory, as well as interfering with the logistic support for the military effort.

In addition, Western reticence gradually eased, as it seemed unfair to expect Ukraine to take so much punishment while denying it means of defence. After Russian forces evacuated the city of Kherson, for example, they moved to the other bank of the Dnipro River and began to shell the city regularly, out of range of any counter-fire. In May 2023, the United Kingdom sent the Storm Shadow cruise missile, followed later by its French equivalent – both of which have ranges of up to 300 kilometres – while the United States abandoned its bar on countries sending Ukraine F-16 aircraft, although these were not expected to be in service until the spring of 2024.

The contrast between the two sides has been further accentuated as Russia has used up its more accurate munitions and experienced soldiers and so becomes more restricted in its ability to manoeuvre, while Ukraine is able to attack military-relevant targets with greater lethality. Here, Ukraine has benefited from access to Western systems, many quite advanced when compared with their Russian counterparts, along with appropriate training and, crucially, intelligence. Ukraine can target Russian assets behind the front line, such as command posts, ammunition dumps, and troop concentrations. Russia has few options other than to rely on artillery barrages designed to render towns and cities indefensible, so that even success means that they end up occupying depopulated rubble. Russia might have preferred to win early with a classical military operation, but as soon as it faced serious resistance, it had no compunctions about attacking residential areas.

The Russo-Ukrainian war therefore allows us to assess a major war between two modern armed forces locked in an intense struggle, but also to contrast the very distinctive approaches adopted by the two sides. Both Russia and Ukraine have had to put their countries on a war footing to stay in the fight.

For both, it has become increasingly 'total', all-consuming in the demands placed on the economy and society. What has been different is the extent to which these have been targeted. This raises the question of whether a total war approach has been strategically counter-productive, whatever the harm imposed tactically.

CHAPTER 2

Strategic choices

The challenge of strategy at times of war is to align means with ends, both of which will be affected by the course of the war. The initial political purpose of a war will reflect the underlying dispute, but as forces are committed to a conflict, issues of reputation and commitment come to the fore. Thus, once a military investment has been made, the stakes in the outcome rise almost automatically. The consequences of trying and failing to resolve a dispute by military means can be greater than not having tried at all.

A country embarking on a war should have confidence that the resources available for investment will be sufficient to meet the war aims. It is, of course, often the case that this confidence is based on faulty calculations. Once the length of a war exceeds the planning assumptions on which it was launched, then there will be a developing tension between ends and means. The sufficiency of the available resources depends in part on the ease by which they can be augmented and replaced, either through production at home or with the help of external suppliers, and in part on those of the enemy. It may not matter so much if resources are being used up faster than they can be replaced if the enemy's resources are being used up quicker. A campaign in trouble may require that aims be scaled back and negotiated compromises sought, leading to a ceasefire that might be combined with, or lead to, a longer-term peace settlement. Sometimes it may even be possible to achieve more than expected. This can be the heady prospect facing a state that is achieving its military objectives faster than first anticipated. It is not always the case that as war aims become more expansive there are fewer means to achieve them. Assuming that matters are not settled in the first days of fighting, wars tend to pass through stages as both sides realign means with ends.

This chapter considers six stages of the Russo-Ukrainian war:

1. The first month of war, covering Russia's invasion and its failure to take Kyiv, which led to the decision to withdraw forces from the north and south to concentrate on the Donbas. This meant

a contraction of Russia's original war aims of controlling the whole country.

2. The period from April to July 2022, when Russian forces sought to take all of Luhansk and Donetsk, making only limited progress.

3. The period from July to September 2022, as Ukraine took the initiative, first using more precise Western artillery to take out key assets such as ammunition dumps and command posts, and then to mount a counter-offensive, which led to Russian forces being pushed out of Kharkiv Oblast and some of Kherson.

4. The period from October 2022 to January 2023. After the setbacks of the previous stage, there was a major Russian strategic reappraisal, which led to expanded war aims, including the annexation of all the territory currently or close to being held by Russian forces, full mobilisation to ease troop shortages, and a more deliberate campaign to take out Ukraine's critical infrastructure.

5. The period from January to May 2023, as the Russians moved to a new offensive before the arrival of further Western weaponry promised to Ukraine that was more suitable for manoeuvre warfare.

6. The period from May 2023, beginning with the failure of Russia's winter offensive and the start of a Ukrainian counter-offensive.

During all these stages, Ukrainian war aims were reasonably constant – to get Russian forces to withdraw from its territory. The only issue was whether, if a compromise peace was available, it would insist on going back to the borders set at the end of 1991 when the Soviet Union broke up, or those of 23 February 2022, when Crimea was firmly in Russian hands and two enclaves in the Donbas were under Russian control. Ukraine's formal position was that it intended to go back to the 1991 borders.

Russian objectives for the war were set by President Putin, who launched it with little consultation except for his closest courtiers. The underlying reason was a long-held conviction that the post-Soviet separation of Ukraine from Russia was unnatural, and that Moscow's hegemony must be restored. The stated reasons for action were claims, held with what conviction it is unclear, that Ukraine was turning into a hostile state, run by Nazis, close to joining NATO, and threatening Russian-language speakers in eastern Ukraine, especially those in the Donbas.

The most controversial claim, because it gained some support among critics of Western policy, such as Professor John Mearsheimer,[5] was that the expansion of NATO after the end of the Cold War created progressively more severe security concerns for Russia.

The door was kept open for possible Ukrainian (and Georgian) accession to NATO at the 2008 Bucharest Summit, although there was insufficient support for early membership then and little in evidence thereafter. The popular movement of 2013–14 that led to the flight of President Viktor Yanukovich (known now in Ukraine as the Revolution of Dignity) was prompted by Russian pressure to abandon a proposed association agreement with the European Union (EU), not NATO. It was this evidence of successful popular protest that probably alarmed Putin as much as anything else, and led to his drastic moves at the time, notably the seizure of Crimea and the sponsorship of rebellions in eastern Ukraine. Those rebellions led to the formation of enclaves in Donetsk and Luhansk, which Putin at the time saw as a means of sustaining pressure on Kyiv, which is why he did not attempt to annex them.[6] Frustration at Kyiv's refusal to have anything to do with these enclaves may have added to Putin's view that their independence needed to be formalised.

Three distinct Russian objectives were therefore present in the period leading up to the war and when it was launched: regime change and installing a friendly government in Kyiv; demilitarisation and neutrality, so no membership of NATO or the EU; and recognition of the claims of Luhansk and

Donetsk People's Republics to be treated as independent entities. From 2014, there was a tension between the objective of keeping Ukraine together so long as it was friendly to Russia, and partitioning Ukraine, taking out those bits assumed to be more naturally Russian. In June 2022, this was resolved: speaking of Peter the Great's acquisition of land from Sweden, Putin observed, 'he seized nothing; he reclaimed it!', adding that, 'It seems it has fallen to us, too, to reclaim and strengthen.'[7]

The variety of potential aims and the underlying tensions have led to the fluctuation of priorities during the war. In the days leading up to the war, Russia stressed the creation of new states out of the two parts of the Donbas, and Ukrainian neutrality. When the war began, the objective was the 'demilitarisation' and 'denazification' of Ukraine, which meant regime change to turn Ukraine into a client state. The failure to achieve this goal meant that for the second stage, Moscow re-emphasised the original objectives with regard to the Donbas. By the third stage, it was seeking to incorporate much of eastern and southern Ukraine into the Russian Federation.

Neither side had allies fighting with them. Early on, there was speculation that Belarus, whose territory provided one of the staging posts for the invasion, might commit forces to the Russian side, but such a move was evidently unpopular within Belarus, and this remained no more than a threat, tying down some Ukrainian forces. No Western states offered to enter the war on Ukraine's side. Putin made it clear that any direct intervention by NATO countries on Ukraine's side would risk serious escalation, and even nuclear war.

NATO countries did, however, supply Ukraine with equipment, starting with defensive systems in the build-up to the war, then moving on to artillery pieces and air defences, and eventually infantry fighting vehicles, tanks, and cruise missiles with relatively modern aircraft in prospect. The pace of decisions to pass on these capabilities and then their delivery has shaped Ukrainian strategy. Russia has largely had to supply itself from its own resources, although it has bought large numbers of drones from Iran.

Options, therefore, opened up for Ukrainian strategy during the course of the war as additional capabilities became available, although Ukraine was hampered by ammunition shortages and the loss of experienced personnel during the more attritional phases of the war. Russian options narrowed, with severe equipment losses and stocks of missiles, rockets, and shells being run down faster than the defence industry could fill the gaps. The most serious issues have come with troop shortages. After September

2022, these eased but the lack of training of the mobilised forces shaped the ways they could be used.

To consider how these factors have affected the strategic choices of both sides, we will now examine the six stages of the war thus far.

STAGE ONE: THE INVASION

Russia's initial strategy was shaped by its desire to turn Ukraine into a puppet state. This was not combined with a total war approach because Moscow expected to win the war through a successful military offensive, largely organised on classical lines, and it would need all of Ukraine's infrastructure for post-war purposes. The strategy was shaped by Putin's underlying beliefs that Ukraine was an artificial state led by an illegitimate government with little popular support. It assumed that Ukraine would crumble quickly in the face of the first Russian onslaught. Considerable effort went into destabilising and subverting Ukraine in the period leading up to the war, relying on sympathetic figures in key positions in Ukraine. These figures both provided advice on Ukraine's readiness for war and were in positions to cooperate with invading forces. This preparatory work appears to have led to misleading and complacent assessments of the readiness and ability of the Ukrainians to fight. There were instances of Russian agents facilitating the invasion but not enough to achieve the most strategic objective – taking the capital, Kyiv.

The strategy required surprise and rapid results. The schedule allowed for the invasion to be completed in ten days and to be followed by six months of occupation to prepare for Ukraine's incorporation into Russia. Central to the plan's success was the early seizure of Kyiv to neutralise the government. The Russian general staff relied on this neutralisation, combined with its overwhelming advantage in deployed forces, to demoralise any Ukrainian resistance.

The plan went awry on the first day. The Russians were caught by the familiar problems with surprise attacks. Strict operational security meant that details of the plan were withheld from those tasked with implementing it until the last minute. Russian forces were unprepared for what they were about to face. When things began to go wrong, there was little capacity to adjust. Too much had been gambled on the first move. The political assumptions informing the invasion were naïve, both in the expectation that killing or capturing the leadership would cow the population, and a general underestimation of the readiness of Ukrainians to fight back. According to the UK think tank, the Royal United Services Institute (RUSI):

For reasons of operational security, orders were not distributed until 24 hours before the invasion to most units. As a result, Russian troops lacked ammunition, fuel, food, maps, properly established communications, and, most critically, a clear understanding at the tactical level of how their actions fitted into the overall plan. It is not so much the case that tactical Russian commanders are incapable of initiative or mission command, but rather that they lacked the detailed instructions of their commanders' intent or their role within the wider battle plan to make such decisions.[8]

Russia thus embarked on its offensives on too many axes, each with too few forces that soon became overstretched but without the means or situational awareness to shift their focus and modus operandi as they got into difficulties.

These problems, which flowed from the requirements of surprise and the determination to prioritise taking the capital Kyiv, were aggravated by a number of issues specific to Russia's armed forces. Any complex military operation involves a variety of units working together. The Battalion Tactical Group (BTG) is Russia's main combined-arms fighting unit. But the interdependence of elements within each BTG meant that the loss of one could cause disproportionate problems if not replaced. The BTGs also lacked leadership of the sort provided by non-commissioned officers in Western armies, systems for sharing information, and candid reporting when operations were going poorly.

The need for speed led Russian forces to rely on the road network, bypassing early pockets of resistance. And while they attacked the obvious fixed targets with their initial air and missile strikes – air defences, command and control infrastructure, airfields, and ammunition storage depots – these attacks provided only limited tactical support to ground forces. The defending Ukrainian units were outgunned, but they had combat experience and strong leadership at junior levels, having been fighting in and around the Donbas since 2014. They were mobile, understood their tasks, and were fighting on familiar territory.

The Ukrainian government was surprised by the scope and scale of the Russian attack, despite Kyiv being warned by both the United States and the United Kingdom that an invasion was imminent. But that did not mean Ukraine was completely unprepared. Its arsenals had been boosted by defensive systems received from Western countries, such as anti-armour and air defence weapons, including large numbers of man-portable air defence systems (MANPADS). On the day before the invasion, vital assets, including air defence systems and aircraft, had been moved away from vulnerable positions so that they survived. Russia's air force, therefore, failed to achieve command of the air and was hampered by persistent Ukrainian air defences while, away from the south where there were significant advances, its land forces were held by dogged and agile Ukrainian troops. Ukrainian individuals not yet called up provided intelligence about Russian movements before taking up arms. Russian supply lines became attenuated and vulnerable to interdiction. Elite units were cut down and large amounts of equipment lost.

The failure to take Kyiv was a major blow to the Russians and framed much of the battle to come. Plans to abduct or kill President Volodymyr Zelensky were thwarted. He refused to be evacuated, and he demonstrated to the Ukrainian people that he could continue leading the country. From the start, he was clear that if other states wished to support his country but would not provide direct military assistance, then they must keep Ukraine supplied ('I don't need a ride, I need ammunition'). Zelensky turned into an energetic and eloquent leader. Taking advantage of the faltering Russian offensive and the fact that communications networks were still functioning, he mobilised Ukrainian society and international support. This meant Russia faced tougher sanctions and Ukraine got more financial and military backing than would otherwise have been the case. Western governments that might have been prepared to limit their responses if Russia had been able to steamroll Ukrainian forces now accepted that they had a duty and an opportunity to support Ukraine.

With its forces over-extended and suffering badly, the Russian Ministry of Defence announced on 25 March 2022 that it would withdraw from the Kyiv, Chernihiv, and Sumy oblasts. In the south and east, it had made much more progress, helped by easier logistics and in some cases collusion between local authorities and the invading forces. Russia, therefore, announced that the new focus would be on the Donbas. This was the first strategic reappraisal.

STAGE TWO: THE DONBAS FOCUS

Having been defeated in the battle for Kyiv, but still holding a substantial chunk of Ukrainian territory, Russia had an opportunity to explore a negotiated settlement. Instead, Putin sought to concentrate on seizing the land that had been at the heart of his political strategy in the period leading up to the invasion. This was described as an 'act of goodwill' in the light of negotiations then underway. Later, Putin would claim that a deal had been close at this stage.

He might have thought that not actively seeking the overthrow of the Zelensky government and allowing Ukrainian membership of the EU was a fair trade for a commitment to neutrality and confirmation that Russia could control the Donbas and keep Crimea (in September 2022, Putin escalated his demands to include even more Ukrainian territory). Ukraine was prepared to consider neutrality but would not concede the Donbas. Its position hardened with evidence of the egregious behaviour of Russian troops in towns they had occupied. Thereafter, it demanded a return to the 1991 borders.

Once withdrawn from northern Ukraine, Russian forces were rushed into new offensive operations before they had a chance to recover from the mauling experienced during the first month of the war. The losses and stress were starting to show. Continuing struggles to cope with the intensity of the fighting had a deleterious effect on morale, with reports of units refusing to return to Ukraine after the late-March retreat. Russia had already committed some 80 per cent of its BTGs. Now it had to turn to other units that would not normally be assigned a central military role, such as the national guard (Rosgvardia). Other units were transferred from Kaliningrad and South Ossetia. The first is the Russian territory between Poland and Lithuania, the base of the Baltic

Fleet, vulnerable to being cut off from the rest of Russia in the event of a confrontation with NATO. The second is a small Russian-backed territory that claims autonomy from Georgia.

With forces well below required levels, the obvious remedy was mass mobilisation, but Putin was not yet prepared to take such a drastic step, given its expected unpopularity and his promise of a limited 'special military operation'. To provide the extra numbers, there was an active campaign to recruit volunteers. Men from the occupied parts of Luhansk and Donetsk were press-ganged into service, and they provided cannon fodder. In addition, the private Wagner Group, which recruited mercenaries, began to play an increasingly prominent role.

While Russian forces were tired, demoralised, and depleted in equipment and number, morale on the Ukrainian side was high, and the Donbas was the area where they had prepared best for a Russian offensive. Their problem was that they were already short on ammunition suitable for their largely Soviet-era artillery. The urgent need for more supplies dominated President Zelensky's diplomacy. Constant pressure was exerted to turn goodwill into deliveries, but this always meant that there was a lag, so Ukrainian forces consistently fought at a material disadvantage.

From late April to June, Russian tactics were reminiscent of those followed in the Chechen wars, with an uncompromising approach to taking key cities, even at a high cost in civilian lives and property. This was first evident in the fight for Mariupol, which dominated the early headlines. As a key port city situated on the Sea of Azov, Mariupol had a large population that could not escape easily once fighting began. There were high civilian casualties as apartment blocks were hit. Ukrainian defenders took a heavy toll of Russian forces, keeping the fight going until late May, at which point Ukrainian forces had no option but to surrender.

Then came the battle for Severodonetsk in Luhansk Oblast. Again, the method was to wear down the defenders through constant artillery barrages, backed by occasional infantry charges, forcing the Ukrainians to retreat until there was nowhere for them to go. Owing to losses in previous battles, Russia had insufficient infantry, which added to their dependence on artillery and to the length of the battles. To force the defenders to reveal their positions, second-class troops, in this case conscripts from LNR and DNR (Russian-sponsored militias based in Luhansk and Donetsk), were used to mount assaults that could be followed up with precise artillery fire and attacks by more elite units.

The battle raised an issue that had been present with Mariupol and that would later emerge in even sharper form in Bakhmut: whether to trade valuable space for essential time. Withdrawing from an exposed position in good order increases the chances of mounting a stronger defence in more favourable conditions. In the first days of the war, Ukraine had little choice in this matter. It needed to defend the big cities of Kyiv and Kharkiv, but there was no point making a stand much beyond their outskirts because of the risk of being encircled or becoming so depleted that there was little left in reserve for the time when they dare not retreat further. Now the calculation was more delicate. Absorbing Russian punches in these cities came at a heavy cost. This was when Kyiv spoke of taking 100–200 casualties per day, troops Ukraine could ill afford to lose.[9] But now, the Ukrainians needed the time. The longer the Russians were held up taking these cities, the more time the Ukrainians had to get vital equipment from the West. These battles also illuminated the consequences of inferior firepower and added to the urgency of getting in Western systems that would boost Ukrainian firepower, a point Zelensky made at every opportunity.

As defence analysts Rob Lee and Michael Kofman observed:

Russia expended valuable manpower and artillery ammunition, while Ukraine pursued a defense-in-depth strategy. By September, NATO arms deliveries had reduced Russia's critical advantage in artillery and Moscow didn't have sufficient forces or ammunition to hold the territory occupied, which set the stage for Ukraine's successful offensives.[10]

The battle for the Donbas bled the Russian military of manpower at a time when it lacked the forces both to hold captured territory and continue offensives. The Russian military offset this deficit by dramatically increasing its rate of artillery fire. This burned through Russia's second-most critical resource, artillery ammunition. The last success of the Russian Donbas campaign came when Lysychansk was taken at the beginning of July 2022. The lack of forces capable of conducting manoeuvre warfare meant that even when there were breakthroughs, they could not be properly exploited. This kept the Russian advance slow, grinding, and costly. The battle for Bakhmut in Donetsk had already begun, even as attention started to shift to the possibility of a Ukrainian offensive.

STAGE THREE: UKRAINE TAKES THE INITIATIVE

Artillery had become the critical constraint on Ukraine's ability to fight back. It was out-gunned to a ratio of ten to one and was using old Soviet-era systems with 152-millimetre artillery rounds. The NATO standard is 155 millimetres. Other former Warsaw Pact countries rummaged through their stocks, but there were limits to how much more could be found. Ukraine needed modern artillery with more precise munitions.

Belatedly, there was a response. In late June, the first pieces reached the front lines, including French Caesar truck-mounted howitzers, which can launch attacks and move away with great speed, and the US M142 High Mobility Artillery Rocket System (HIMARS), with a range of 70 kilometres. These not only had twice the range of the old systems but pinpoint accuracy. This was the start of a process that, to somewhat over-simplify, saw the Russians – reliant on overwhelming numbers and raw power, with replacement equipment of older vintage and lower quality – becoming more of a twentieth-century army while the Ukrainians became more of a twenty-first-century force. The transition would take time, but it held out the prospect, which influenced all subsequent calculations, of an eventual Ukrainian force qualitatively if not quantitatively superior to that of the Russian.

Improved Ukrainian artillery caused serious problems for the Russian military effort straight away. Although it was no secret that these systems were coming, the Russian high command failed to consider the implications for Russia's logistical and command systems, and in particular the role of large ammunition depots close to the front lines. The Ukrainians wasted little time in mounting a series of attacks on these dumps, significantly reducing the Russian rate of fire and forcing a move to a more inefficient logistics system, with supplies being kept further back. In addition, the Russian command network was targeted, with a couple of divisional headquarters being taken out. Ukraine's improved counter-battery fire added to the new complications facing Russian forces. Lastly, Ukraine's air defences were able to protect these systems while safeguarding Ukraine's own supply lines.

Russia was now starting to think defensively about how best to hold its positions in the face of potential Ukrainian counter-offensives. The Ukrainians spoke openly of plans to retake Kherson, one of the most important cities taken by Russia and without much of a fight, in an area vital to the economy but also to the defence of Odesa and, potentially, to any effort to retake Crimea. Aware of this, Russia continued to do enough in the

Donbas to tie Ukrainian forces down, while moving forces from Izyum in Kharkiv and elsewhere to reinforce its position in Kherson. This left Russian positions north of the Donbas under-strength in both manpower and equipment. A number of stopgap measures were put in place, which meant units found themselves in positions for which they were quite unsuited. Much attention was given to the efforts by Wagner to recruit in Russian prisons, offering eventual freedom in return for time spent on the front lines. None of this could compensate for the fact that Russia lacked the forces for an extended front line.

Many observers, including in Russia, noted that a potential Ukrainian offensive force was gathering close to Kharkiv, but by now the Russians lacked the capacity to reinforce a threatened area of the front. Compared to the earlier Russian offensives, Ukraine's was well planned, with artillery preparing the ground, infantry and armour punching their way through, and air defences providing protection. Breakthroughs were achieved in areas thinly held by below-strength units with poorly trained troops unable to cope with a serious offensive. Ukrainian forces rapidly advanced to Kupyansk and then Izyum, forcing Russian forces to withdraw from both towns and most of Kharkiv Oblast.

The situation in Kherson was quite different. Here, the Ukrainians could employ the same types of forces available for Kharkiv, but Russian defences were deep, extensive, and prepared. The terrain was also more open, so Ukrainian forces could be spotted by Russian unmanned aerial vehicles (UAVs) and hit with artillery. The main problem Russia faced in the defence of Kherson city was keeping forces supplied, especially as Ukraine attacked the bridges over the Dnipro River.

The Kharkiv retreat led to a crisis in Russia as critics from the right, convinced of the necessity of the war but furious at its conduct, assigned blame. They observed how much Ukrainian forces had benefited from an inflow of advanced weaponry, their competence in combined arms, and their mobility, allowing them to avoid costly urban battles. Russian troops were portrayed as fighting valiantly. The failures lay in coordination between units in Kharkiv, many of which were unprepared to deal with a situation of this sort and lacked sufficient artillery, air, and intelligence support. The main blame was directed at the senior figures in Moscow – Defence Minister Sergei Shoigu and Chief of the General Staff Valery Gerasimov.

A low point for Putin came at a conference in Uzbekistan. Here could be seen Russia's isolation, even among countries expected to be more sympathetic. Central Asian states were visibly distancing themselves. Putin was obliged to acknowledge that both China's President Xi Jinping and India's Prime Minister Narendra Modi had concerns about the war. Speaking to the media on 16 September 2022 at the end of the conference, Putin was defensive. Asked about the Ukrainian counter-offensive, he said: 'Let's see how it goes and how it ends.' He stuck with the minimum rather than maximum objectives – 'the liberation of the entire territory of Donbas' – and reported that Russian forces continued with this goal 'despite these counter-offensive attempts by the Ukrainian army'. The 'main task,' he insisted, 'remains unchanged, and it is being implemented'.[11]

If the Ukrainians kept on pressing, including with their 'terrorist attacks' against Russian and Russian-supporting officials in the occupied areas, what he claimed as being a restrained response might be reviewed. Noting that Russia had already delivered 'a couple of sensitive blows' against Ukraine, he added: 'Well, what about that? We will assume that these are warning strikes. If the situation continues to develop in this way, the answer will be more serious.' This indicates that Putin's thinking was already moving to targeting Ukrainian infrastructure as compensation for the difficult situation in the land war. Missile strikes had already caused widespread blackouts in Kharkiv, apparently in response to Ukraine's successful counter-offensive.[12]

STAGE FOUR: RUSSIA'S SECOND REAPPRAISAL

Russia was shocked into a major reassessment of strategy. This was another moment when Putin might have looked for a way to de-escalate the war, but instead he decided to respond to hardline critics from the nationalist right. The cumulative effect was to ensure that the war lasted longer and that a negotiated peace settlement would be even harder to achieve.

The key elements were:

1. *Annexation of the four occupied (or more accurately, semi-occupied) oblasts of Donetsk, Luhansk, Kherson, and Zaporizhzhia*. This raised the stakes, demonstrating that the aim was to expand the borders of Russia. This made it much harder for Moscow to back down as it would mean abandoning Russian territory. Referendums were rushed to legitimise the annexations, all showing an absurd and uniform majority support not far off 100 per cent.

2. *Attacks on infrastructure*. The hardliners had been demanding this for some time. There had been similar attacks all through the war but now, using

combinations of missiles and 'kamikaze drones' supplied by Iran, they would be more systematic and focused. This will be discussed more below.

3. *Introduction of martial law in occupied territories and in some parts of Russia.* This made it easier to control discontent, continue with 'Russification', and mobilise troops for the front.

4. *Authorisation of mass mobilisation.* This was intended to address the military's chronic troop shortages. Some 300,000 were called up initially, of which around 120,000 were moved to the front as a matter of urgency. The problem for the military command was not one of finding the bodies, especially if the authorities were not too choosy, but in clothing, training, and equipping them. Russia was already digging deep into reserves of weapons and equipment, and there were few spare officers available to give instruction. Although the initial mobilisation was something of a shambles, new structures were put in place in late October 2022 so that the process became more efficient.[13]

5. *Appointment of a new 'Commander of the Joint Group of Forces in the Special Military Operation Zone'.* The Russian command structure went through a number of changes before September, but General Sergei Surovikin's appointment was designed to signal a firmer operational grip.

His reputation was that of a tough and harsh commander, as demonstrated in Syria. He had also been involved in the attempted coup against Mikhail Gorbachev in 1991. He served one spell in prison for this and another for arms trafficking. Unsurprisingly, he was the choice of the hard-line nationalist faction, including Wagner boss Yevgeny Prigozhin.

Surovikin's strategy involved a largely defensive approach on land, with more emphasis on attacks on Ukrainian infrastructure, to which considerable resources were devoted:

All measures are taken to build up the combat strength and formations of military units, create additional reserves, equip defence lines and positions along the entire line of contact, [and] continue attacks with high-precision weapons on military facilities and infrastructure facilities . . . to reduce the combat capability [of the Ukrainian troops].[14]

The aim was to use available troops, whether properly trained and equipped or not, to thicken defences at the front. If these lines could be held through the winter, fresh and better trained units might then be ready for more offensive operations.

Surovikin wanted to evacuate Kherson city imme-diately to get troops to more defensible lines. Putin reportedly refused. He eventually agreed, but it was not until November 2022 that Russian troops evacuated from the right bank of the Dnipro. Russia appeared to have conducted a competent withdrawal without sustaining heavy losses.

STAGE FIVE: RENEWED RUSSIAN OFFENSIVE

Ukraine's best strategy was to eliminate Russian capa-bilities where they could be identified and hit with long-range artillery, steadily reducing capabilities and morale, although this by itself would not enable them to retrieve lost territory. One example came during the first minutes of 2023 when a vocational college in Makiivka, close to the city of Donetsk and some 12.5 kilometres from the front line, was hit by Ukrainian artillery. The building housed hundreds of recently conscripted Russian soldiers along with stores of ammunition, which was the main reason so much was obliterated in the blast. The numbers killed ranged from an official count of 89 to an unofficial number of close to 300. Russian commanders blamed it on a lapse of operational security – mobile phones used by soldiers in the facility allowed Ukraine to pick up the target.[15] Even without the phones, how-ever, the deployment was hardly a secret.

Nor was this an isolated incident. There were other reports of buildings housing troops being hit. After the summer losses, Russia had dispersed vital assets and kept them to the rear if possible, but this led to inefficiencies, aggravated by the winter weather, when it came to bringing them together for combat purposes. And troops were needed at the front.

This appears to have led to yet another reappraisal marked by the demotion of Surovikin on 11 January 2023 and Valery Gerasimov, Chief of the General Staff, being put in charge of the overall operation. Putin was apparently frustrated by the defensive posture and demanded more offensive operations. Otherwise, how could he meet his objectives, which required that more territory in the partly occupied oblasts be taken to give their annexation some credibility?

Russia's forces had persevered with their single serious offensive operation – to take Bakhmut in Donetsk. This became the latest in a series of epic encounters, along with Mariupol and Severodonetsk, in which the Russians spent months and suffered heavy casualties trying to take cities they considered strategic but which were depopulated and reduced to rubble. Ukrainian forces thwarted the Russian attacks but at a high cost. President Zelensky visited the city on 20 December 2022, a time when it appeared in peril. The day after, Ukrainian forces mounted a counter-attack and forced Russian troops to withdraw from some areas. But this remained a back-and-forth battle. The Russians took the adjacent town of Soledar, adding to the pressure on the Ukrainian side. In all of this, Wagner losses were huge. Their commanders did not appear to care as they pushed troops forward to the Ukrainian lines. Meanwhile, Prigozhin complained that he was being denied artillery shells because the Ministry of Defence's priorities lay elsewhere.

By now, Ukraine and its Western supporters had been through their own strategic reappraisal. Putin was not going to abandon the war quickly, yet Ukraine lacked the capabilities to embark on a major offensive of its own. In January 2023, the Americans led a significant effort to put together a package of weapons that would support a substantial offensive. The assessment was that only a convincing defeat in battle might shock the Russian leadership into seeking a way out of the war.

Promises were made to send French AMX-10 RC armoured reconnaissance vehicles, US Bradley and German Marder infantry fighting vehicles, Stryker armoured personnel carriers, air defence systems, and tens of thousands of rockets and artillery rounds, as well as UK Brimstone missiles, French-made Caesar howitzers from Denmark, and Sweden's Archer artillery system. Then came main battle tanks, first UK Challengers and then US Abrams, but with German-made Leopards making up the largest number.

A statement from nine of the suppliers explained the rationale:

> We recognise that equipping Ukraine to push Russia out of its territory is as important as equipping them to defend what they already have. Together we will continue supporting Ukraine to move from resisting to expelling Russian forces from Ukrainian soil.[16]

The commitment of NATO countries to a Ukrainian victory still had its limits, set by anxieties about nuclear escalation, much to the frustration of President Zelensky, who wanted combat aircraft. Ukrainians persevered with all their requests because they could see a pattern of initial resistance followed by growing sympathy and eventual, though belated, acquiescence.

The other problem was the time it would take for the promised equipment to have an impact, as it would have to be delivered to Ukraine and be integrated into its forces. There were big logistical issues – transporting these heavy systems and all the kit that goes with them, including ammunition, was a major undertaking.

The Ukrainians had been waiting for Western governments to catch up with the logic of the military situation and of their political commitments. In their battles, they were still usually out-gunned, coping with old and often worn-out equipment, and taking casualties even if they inflicted far more on the Russians. The need to make the most of their new capabilities argued for postponing action until their offensive units were fully kitted out and ready to go. That meant, however, leaving the initiative to the enemy.

The Russians could work out the Ukrainian timetable as well as anyone else. Moscow's timetable was different. The country was on a war footing and the systems for mobilisation were in place, having recovered from the organisational chaos of the first weeks. Russia could replenish losses, and was doing so continually, even if with inadequately trained and poorly motivated troops. Defence production had been ramped up to ensure new supplies of equipment and ammunition, even if not quite making up for what had been and was still being lost. Russia was getting ready for a long war.

Yet Putin was also frustrated with the state of the war, as his territorial objectives had not been achieved. This is why Surovikin was demoted and the ever-loyal Gerasimov put in charge. There were then some 320,000 Russian troops in occupied Ukraine, many newly mobilised. Ukrainian intelligence suggested that Putin had ordered all of Donetsk and Luhansk to be seized by the end of March. If so, he was disappointed.

Part of the Russian military tradition was to acknowledge weaknesses and develop workarounds, making do with what was available, and persevering despite heavy losses. In addition to the regular units of the army, the marines, and the interior forces, there had been an influx of 'mobiks' (recently mobilised troops), along with what was left of the 'People's Militias' of the Donetsk and Luhansk People's Republics, the Chechens and Cossacks, plus the mercenaries of Wagner and other private military companies. So, there was still no true unity of command, and there was evidence of unhappiness in the ranks, low morale, fratricide, poor coordination, and unimaginative tactics. Yet the army did not fall apart. Soldiers continued to be used as a cheap resource, with the more expendable sent against Ukrainian lines, with a gun at their back if they were tempted to retreat, sacrificed to help reveal the location of Ukrainian forces so that they could be better targeted by artillery, as well as exhausting the defenders so that they were less able to cope when the expendables were replaced by more professional and better equipped units.

After huge losses, Russia depended in many areas on old equipment suffering from wear and tear. They were unable to manoeuvre in large formations, especially in winter. Offensives tend to be associated with the spring, when the ground hardens and trees provide a degree of cover. The air force was occasionally active but inhibited by Ukrainian air defences. Most independent analysts agreed with the Washington-based Institute for the Study of War that 'Russian military command may be rushing to launch a large-scale offensive operation to conquer Donetsk Oblast in an unrealistic timeframe and likely without sufficient combat power.'[17] It was hard to see how they could manage swift and effective movements to catch Ukrainian defenders unawares and smash through their lines.

When Putin spoke on 21 February 2023, days before the first anniversary of the invasion, he described a war that was as much against NATO as Ukraine, and for which he had no obvious strategy. 'Step by step,' he said, 'carefully and consistently we will deal with the tasks we have at hand.' How many steps and how long this would take he did not say. He talked in much more detail about support to the families of 'fallen fighters', 'long-term home care, and high-technology prosthetics' for the badly wounded, and then, for those currently fighting, 'a leave of absence of at least 14 days every six months'. Meanwhile, 'the latest technology' will 'ensure high-quality standards in the Army and Navy . . . Our goal is to start mass production. This work is underway and is picking up pace.' He was describing a new normal for Russia that offered indefinite war.[18]

The Russian offensive achieved little. Vuhledar was attacked in late January, adding to the continuing battle for Bakhmut, with other attacks directed against Marinka, Avdiivka, and Kreminna. Vuhledar turned out to be catastrophic for two regular marine (Naval Infantry) brigades as they advanced over a relatively open landscape, their vehicles and troops spotted while their tanks travelled over heavily mined fields. With so much equipment lost and such heavy costs, this attack fizzled out.

Bakhmut remained the focus. Wagner, with assistance from Russian regulars, moved forward after taking Soledar and then the high ground to Bakhmut's north and south. The imminent seizure of the city was soon being spoken of as a vital next step for Russia. Defence Minister Shoigu explained that Bakhmut was an important hub of the Ukrainian armed forces.[19] So long as Putin wanted all of the Donbas, Bakhmut had to be taken.

As the Ukrainian position became more parlous, the loss of Bakhmut appeared a distinct possibility. There was talk of withdrawal before it became too late. On 6 March 2023, Zelensky insisted that this would not happen, and, lest there be any doubt, that he had the backing of the country's senior commanders in this view.

Then followed one of the sharpest debates yet seen on the wisdom of Ukrainian strategy. At its heart was the sort of morbid cost-benefit analysis unavoidably involved in assessments of military strategy when every course of action carries risks and the prospect of high losses. Put simply, the question was whether the costs, in terms of lives lost and ammunition expended, were worth it when it came to denying Russia a long-sought victory. Zelensky's critics worried that, at best, the loss of Bakhmut would be delayed, but with a higher risk of casualties, especially if the Russians were able to encircle the defending forces before they could escape. *The Washington Post* reported in mid-March:

The quality of Ukraine's military force, once considered a substantial advantage over Russia, has been degraded by a year of casualties that have taken many of the most experienced fighters off the battlefield, leading some Ukrainian officials to question

Kyiv's readiness to mount a much-anticipated spring offensive.[20]

Against the prudent view that evacuation would be the best course, Zelensky was reluctant to cede any more territory to the Russians unless there was no other choice. One issue was the comparable rates of attrition, with suggestions that for every Ukrainian casualty there were five Russian. But as the Ukrainians were put more onto the back foot, this advantage was being reduced. The trade did not look so good when experienced Ukrainian fighters were lost in return for Russian 'expendables'. Nor would the evacuation inevitably lead to Russia moving quickly down the roads to Kramatorsk and Slovyansk. The Ukrainians could fall back to lines that would be easier to defend.

In the end, Zelensky's judgement was as much political as military. As with other cities fought over in similar ways, the operational consequences of a loss could be argued over, but after such a hard fight, losing Bakhmut would be a political blow. More to the point, denying Russia victory in Bakhmut would be an even more severe blow to Moscow if it left Russian forces unable to advance further into Donetsk. The Ukrainians managed to keep their limited supply routes into Bakhmut open, and mounted some counter-attacks to relieve the pressure. By the start of May, the city had still not been taken. Prigozhin blamed Wagner's heavy losses and slow progress on a continuing conspiracy by the Ministry of Defence to deny him ammunition. These arguments became so bitter that it seemed as if Wagner was using the episode to become the champion of Russia's frustrated ultra-nationalists.

By the end of the month, the battered city was under Wagner's control, ready to be handed over to the Russian army. But it was a pointless victory because there was no viable city left to be 'Russified', and by this time Ukrainian forces had regained some territory flanking the city, meaning it could not serve as a staging post for further Russian advances. In addition, Russian forces were now shifting to a more defensive posture.

The Russian offensive had achieved little more than a few villages plus Bakhmut. The prospect of a Ukrainian counter-offensive was now starting to prey on the minds of Russia's commanders. Six months after Putin had doubled down on expanding his war aims and put his country onto a full war footing, Russian forces had made negligible progress. Ukraine was preparing for the next stage.

STAGE SIX: UKRAINE'S COUNTER-OFFENSIVE

Among Ukraine's Western supporters, there were concerns that its offensive might be hampered by problems with ammunition stocks and air defences, and the challenges of introducing promised Western equipment into the Ukrainian forces. In leaked documents from February 2023, assessments could be found of significant 'force generation and sustainment shortfalls', the likelihood that the Ukrainian offensive would result in only 'modest territorial gains', and a warning of a 'grinding campaign of attrition' that was 'likely heading toward a stalemate'.[21] By May, however, many of the new systems were in place with training completed. More importantly, the Russian offensive had clearly failed, at an enormous cost in manpower and morale. Pentagon estimates suggested that Russia had taken 100,000 casualties since December (including 20,000 killed). The fighting had also taken a heavy toll on the Ukrainians, with the loss of some of their most experienced troops.

On 29 May 2023, Zelensky told his people that the offensive was ready:

Not only provision of ammunition, not only training of new brigades, not only our tactics. But also deadlines. This is what is most important. A timeline as to how we will move. We will. Decisions have been made. I thank every soldier and sergeant, officer and general, every brigade that has prepared.

The Ukrainians were content to keep Russia guessing about the form the counter-offensive would take. By late May 2023, having spent months repelling Russian attacks, Ukraine saw its opportunity to shape the war's next stage. The shift was marked by several moves, some that would do no more than irritate and embarrass the Kremlin, such as drone attacks against Moscow or sponsoring an anti-Putin Russian militia's raid into the border region of Belgorod. Others, such as taking out Russian assets well behind the front lines, including ammunition and fuel dumps, were designed to degrade Russian logistics, making it harder to reinforce forward positions. Railway lines in Russia were sabotaged. Ukraine was also able to take advantage of the exhaustion of Russian troops in the Bakhmut area, where Russia had yet to strengthen its defences.

But all were seen as sideshows compared to the most important initiatives involving the fresh Ukrainian brigades, kept separate from the recent defensive fights. Western supporters had trained about 63,000 Ukrainian troops and provided more than 150 modern battle tanks, along with many older tanks and infantry fighting vehicles.

The new brigades were deliberately held back from the battle of Bakhmut. General Valery Zaluzhny, Commander-in-Chief of the Armed Forces of Ukraine, acknowledged in December 2022 that the fighters in Bakhmut had been left coping with inadequate ammunition and equipment so that these new brigades could be formed.

May the soldiers in the trenches forgive me, it's more important to focus on the accumulation of resources right now for the more protracted and heavier battles that may begin next year.[22]

It did not require too much time looking at a map to conclude that ideally these new units would be used in an offensive push that would start in Zaporizhzhia, move through the middle of the occupied territories, and then on to the Sea of Azov, dividing Russia's forces and putting its hold over Crimea at risk.

The Russian general staff looked at the same maps and prepared their defences accordingly, with layers of mines, anti-tank traps and barriers, trenches and artillery that would all need to be overcome. Without air superiority, there would be no opportunity to create a 'permissive environment', with the enemy so battered by days of strikes that they would be unable to cope once the army moved against them. Russian defences would need to be assaulted directly.

How hard this would be soon became apparent. On 8 June 2023, Ukrainian forces made an early assault close to Mala Tomachka on the Zaporizhzhia front. They got caught by the density of the minefield they were trying to breach, leading to the loss of a number of vehicles.[23] Images of destroyed US-supplied Bradley infantry fighting vehicles were soon being widely circulated by pro-Russian bloggers, celebrating the failure of the Ukrainian offensive almost as soon as it started. On 13 June, Putin, not normally one to comment in detail on operations, felt confident enough to assert that Ukraine had launched a 'massive counter-offensive, using strategic reserves that were prepared for this task', and that had been rebuffed by Russian forces.[24]

Press reporting underlined the difficulties faced by Ukrainian forces, pointing, for example, to improved Russian helicopter capabilities, notably the Ka-52 'Alligator' attack helicopters,[25] and upgraded Lancet drones.[26] President Zelensky acknowledged progress had been 'slower than desired', noting that, 'Some people believe this is a Hollywood movie and expect results now. It's not. What's at stake is people's lives.'[27] His military chief, General Zaluzhny, said something similar: 'It's not a show the whole world is watching and betting on or anything. Every day, every meter is given by blood.'[28]

The problems faced were not surprising. Russian defences were never going to be easy to breach. Known problems such as a lack of air power and de-mining equipment turned out to be as limiting as feared. They were aggravated by a lack of close coordination between advancing units and the artillery required to suppress defences. Once vehicles were disabled at the front of a column, those stuck behind were targeted by Russian fire, whether from artillery, anti-tank missiles, attack helicopters, or drones. All of this was not helped by unusually rainy weather, which kept the ground boggy and hampered mobility. The basic problem was that all large formations were vulnerable once spotted, and with numerous drones flying overhead, the risk of being spotted was high. Once a unit was caught by obstacles, including mines, vulnerability became greater.

After the early June setback, the Ukrainians went back to relying on actions more at platoon and company level, with small groups of soldiers rushing from one tree line to another, or creeping forward to clear a way through a minefield. Russian forces adapted in similar ways, if only to prevent Ukrainians consolidating even limited gains. The challenge for units from either side moving forward was to find positions with some cover that could be held against enemy counters. It rarely made sense to stop in an open field. Fighting became like the ebb and flow of a tide as small settlements regularly changed hands.

As *The Economist* noted, it was possibly never realistic to expect brigades 'put together in a hurry with unfamiliar equipment' and with barely a month of training, to be proficient when it came to 'co-ordinating complex attacks involving multiple units using different sorts of weapons'.[29] Ukrainians were working not only with many different types of equipment, each with their own operational and maintenance issues, but also different philosophies. This was an army with strong Soviet roots that learned to adapt after the Russian enclaves were forged in 2014, and then grew quickly after the full-scale invasion of February 2022 under strong NATO influence. As it grew, many of its most professional soldiers were lost in the intense fighting. Those who survived became increasingly fatigued.

Ukraine also had shortages. The position on artillery shells was eased when South Korea changed its previous stance and agreed to pass on large quantities of 155-millimetre shells. Most controversially, the United States agreed to supply cluster bombs (DPICM – dual-purpose improved conventional munitions).[30] These could be fired from howitzers or

HIMARS, releasing large numbers of small bomblets to cover a wide area, helping the Ukrainians stay in the 'artillery race' and improving their tactical options. Cluster munitions were controversial because, along with mines, they risked a tragic legacy. Unexploded munitions will cause harm to civilians for years to come as battlefields are reclaimed. But old Soviet versions had already been used by both sides. Ukraine made clear that it would confine the use of cluster munitions to Russian military targets – it had no interest in targeting its own civilians. Its top priority was its operational needs.

Franz-Stefan Gady and Michael Kofman noted in February 2023 that the new units would not have enough combat power to allow a NATO-style emphasis on rapid manoeuvre and 'combined arms' operations (close coordination of armour, artillery, and infantry). An attritional phase – centering on artillery to degrade opposing forces – was unavoidable,[31] a view confirmed after a visit to the front lines. Gady and Kofman stressed the difficulties the Ukrainians faced fighting in a combined arms fashion at scale, largely because of deficiencies in training and experience.

Ukrainian soldiers' ability to master Western tech quickly led to misplaced optimism that the time it takes to develop cohesive fighting units could be short-circuited. Putting these units in the vanguard of a difficult assault, instead of more experienced formations, now looks like a mistake that reflected the prioritisation of Western kit over time in the field.

Even if they had been better prepared, the lack of key capabilities would have hampered Ukrainian advances. Gady and Kofman argued that remedying these deficiencies required better equipment and more time. The focus should not be on encouraging Ukraine to follow best Western practice but to help it 'fight the way it fights best' – which meant accepting the logic of attritional warfare.[32]

The UK's Chief of the Defence Staff, Admiral Sir Tony Radakin, described Ukraine's approach as 'starve, stretch, and strike'. *Starve* referred to the regular attacks on Russian logistics and command structures, and *stretch* to the 'multiple axes being probed and feints by Ukraine'. Their aim was to take advantage of the length of the front line, over a thousand kilometres. As each attack required a response, this could lead to the progressive commitment of Russian reserves. *Strike* is what would come next, when the bulk of the twelve fresh and modernised brigades, two-thirds of which were still being held back, could be pushed forward.[33]

In late July, the Ukrainians began to push harder again in the south. A new brigade was brought into the action, taking some of the pressure off the one that had borne the brunt of the fighting, looking to take advantage of a perceived weakness in the Russian lines. But this was still a hard grind. Progress would be slow.[34]

Much would depend on Russian strategy. Russian commanders opted against a passive defence, waiting for the Ukrainians to find a way through the minefields and then overcoming their extensive fortifications, in favour of denying Ukrainian forces any gains at all. Whenever they moved into a village, a counter-attack was soon mounted. This was why the 'stretch' was so important, as the combination of a long front and uncertainty about where the main Ukrainian effort would be launched meant that the Russians would lack depth in individual sectors.

After Ukraine had used the HIMARS multiple rocket launcher to attack Russian ammunition dumps left carelessly close to the front and destroyed many, the Russians sought to keep stores out of range. With the increased tempo of battle, this created a dilemma for Russian commanders. Either ammunition and other supplies must be ferried to the front over long distances, which took time and carried its own risks of interdiction, or else they must be stored closer to the front, where they were vulnerable to direct strikes. The same was true with artillery. Intensive use meant that not only were barrels getting worn and shells expended, but locations were revealed. Artillery units could be struck before they could hide away. Oleksiy Danilov, secretary of Ukraine's National Security and Defence Council, tweeted on 4 July 2023 that 'the number one task' for Ukrainian forces was:

> . . . the maximum destruction of manpower, equipment, fuel depots, armoured personnel carriers, command posts, artillery, and air defence forces of the Russian army. The last days are particularly fruitful. Now a war of destruction is equal to a war of kilometres. More destroyed – more released. The more effective the first, the more the second. We act calmly, measuredly, step by step.[35]

The more Russian forces committed to battle, the less they had for later. Even though most of the Russian counter-attacks were not successful, the objective might simply have been to keep up pressure on Ukraine so that they could not consolidate any gains and had to prepare their own defences. There were also risks for Ukrainian forces if they got stretched. In late July on the eastern front, as

Ukrainian forces were rotated in one area and less experienced troops came in, the Russians advanced a few kilometres – though they had insufficient combat power to take this mini-offensive much further and no obvious objective to take and hold. The Ukrainians stabilised this situation, but it was another example of the fluidity of the battlefield.

Although the toughest fighting was around the southern defensive line, there continued to be substantial fighting around Bakhmut. The city had been taken earlier in the year, with the Wagner Group leading the Russian effort. One important consequence of this battle was the falling out between Wagner's boss, Yevgeny Prigozhin, and Defence Minister Sergei Shoigu over the degree of support being given to the Wagner troops and the conduct of the war more generally. This led to a bizarre mutiny that saw Wagner troops move without resistance to Russia's Southern Command HQ at Rostov-on-Don and then towards Moscow, shooting down helicopters and one aircraft on the way, before agreeing to turn back. Wagner relocated to Belarus. Prigozhin still moved freely in Russia[36] until the inevitable assassination came when his plane was blown up on 23 August. Meanwhile, the most senior military figures close to Wagner were sacked: General Surovikin, responsible for the construction of the southern defensive line, and General Ivan Popov, who denounced the lack of support to front-line troops and pointed to problems with counter-battery fire. Popov complained of being 'hit in the rear by our senior commander, who treacherously and vilely decapitated our army at the most difficult and tense moment'.[37]

If the aim was to ride out the Ukrainian offensive until it ran out of steam and Kyiv's Western supporters started to look for a way out, then the Russian strategy was curious. It was not fighting in such a way as to conserve its strength for a long haul. Instead, it threw as much as possible into the battles. It was true that Russia had stepped up defence production, but this was barely keeping pace with use. There was little capacity left. Russia was moving units from other parts of the country,[38] demonstrating that Ukraine had now become the Kremlin's overriding priority, even though this left it less able to cope with emergencies elsewhere.

By late August 2023, the position had not quite reached a stalemate, as Ukraine was making slow but steady gains, although not on the scale it had hoped. Both sides were struggling in their own way and taking casualties. Neither was inclined to abandon the fight. The war had become a test of endurance. As noted earlier, such wars are described as attritional because they can only be won if the enemy army collapses through depletion and exhaustion. Western military theory prefers manoeuvre warfare, leading to territory being seized and victory imposed. Attrition had come to be disparaged as an inferior and undesirable form of warfare. Yet the lack of dash and drama in attritional warfare does not mean that it cannot offer a route to victory, either by creating the conditions for manoeuvre or by forcing the enemy to recognise that its position can only get worse. A long war requires more careful pacing and puts demands on Ukraine's supporters to keep it supplied with equipment and ammunition.

There was always a degree of mythology in the emphasis on the potential of manoeuvre. US successes in the conventional stages of wars tended to be the result of superior firepower as superior manoeuvre. Enemy forces could not cope with the fire directed at them, whether from air strikes, cruise missiles, artillery, or tanks. Facing an enemy with sufficient firepower means any advance risks casualties and equipment losses. As Mick Ryan has observed:

Every military activity features attrition. Even in peacetime, military organisations suffer attrition through training injuries, poor retention and bad equipment maintenance. This is magnified in war by combat losses, injuries and sickness as well as psychological injury.[39]

'Attrition' therefore describes what regularly happens in war. It is not really a type of war or even a distinctive strategy.

The stakes were high. Should the Ukrainian offensive follow the Russian into failure, then the prospect was of a continuing stalemate, with another harsh winter of fighting and energy shortages looming. International calls for a ceasefire, preferably accompanied by a full peace settlement, would grow louder. Gradually, Western governments realised that it was unwise to pin everything on a single offensive. They began to demonstrate long-term commitment by approving arms packages and promising sustainability over time, signalling to Putin that it would be misguided to rely on outlasting the Ukrainians in the fight.

The value of any offensive would depend not only on the ground taken but the effect on Russian attitudes. One view was that Putin could continue with this war indefinitely because he remained firmly in charge and could not countenance defeat. Yet Russian strategy has been through several shifts and turns during the war and might do so again, especially if the elite became convinced of the futility of the war and the fragility of Russia's occupation.

THE CONDUCT OF LAND WARFARE

The lessons for land warfare drawn from Russia's invasion were not surprising. Many were timeless. Geography, climate, and the seasons of the year matter. Rivers form natural boundaries and forests can provide a degree of cover. When the ground turns boggy, movement is impeded. Extreme cold undermines the performance of soldiers. Cities are apt to be largely destroyed in fighting, but because of urbanisation, cities are becoming harder to avoid.

Logistics are the key to sustaining any operation. If supply lines are vulnerable to disruption or interdiction, this can soon undermine front-line operations. Once two sides get locked in artillery duels, then ammunition gets used up at rates that far exceed pre-war planning, while equipment, if it is not destroyed or disabled by enemy action, will soon show signs of wear and tear because of the intensity with which it is being used. The efficient use of ammunition gradually becomes a major preoccupation.

Defence is the stronger form of warfare. Offensives prosper only where they are limited and well prepared. Russian gains came during the first days of the war when they had the advantage of surprise and were able to move fast. Yet in the north, they took forward positions that could not be sustained and soon got into trouble against agile Ukrainian units and had to withdraw. In the south, they met less resistance, especially where defences were poorly organised, notably in Kherson. In subsequent stages of the war, beginning with the battle for the Donbas, Russian gains were few, covering narrow areas, and achieved only at immense cost and over months.

The most impressive Ukrainian offensive in Kharkiv came when they took advantage of a weak and amateurish defence as the Russian high command were focused on Donetsk and Kherson. Where Russian defences were prepared, and then bolstered by the extra troops generated by mobilisation, Ukrainian offensives also made slow progress. Where defences were unlikely to hold, it could make sense to trade space for time to get to lines that would be much harder for the enemy to break, although that was a move political leaders could find difficult to accept. Where defences could hold, even if not indefinitely, it could be worth attritional battles to prevent breakthroughs while fresh forces were being prepared for counter-offensives.

Another important but familiar lesson was the importance of training and local leadership. The

Ukrainians knew what they were fighting for and, at least early on in the war, had many soldiers with substantial experience in positions to guide local operations. As they were killed or wounded, and as the army grew with more reservists, their influence declined. There were suggestions that old Soviet centralising habits in the Ukrainian command structure died hard, and there may have been some truth in that, but managing larger scale operations and allocating scarce resources, especially ammunition, was bound to encourage centralisation. It is also the case that the better the means of communication, the more opportunities there are for senior officers to try to control all operations from the centre. Ukraine benefited from an educated workforce with many IT specialists, who were able to help with improvisation and adaptation. The urgency of the situation limited the time for training. Fresh troops used for offensive purposes struggled at first to take full advantage of the equipment provided by the West. It was one thing to learn how to drive a tank but another to work out how to use it tactically in combination with other capabilities, or to work out how to navigate a minefield.

Russian command and control varied. Many of the later operations in the Donbas were under the notional control of the LNR and DNR militias, which had very few of their original troops. The commanders were the subject of numerous complaints from the 'mobiks' for being absent and uncaring, threatening those who refused to comply with orders and taking kit and money. Early in the war, the complexity of the operation and the suddenness with which it was launched, and then the lack of operational security as they became dependent on Ukrainian communications networks, meant that senior commanders coped poorly. A lack of realistic exercises against a capable opponent meant they did not fully understand their own capabilities and lacked the tactical nous to get out of difficulties.

There was also something familiar in the debate that developed around the role of tanks. The loss of so many Russian tanks during the early days of the war led commentators to pronounce on their obsolescence. Yet there were several explanations for the losses. One was that the Russian forces failed to follow their own combined arms doctrine – integration of tank forces with infantry, artillery, and intelligence would have left the tanks less exposed. Another was a failure of logistics. About a third of Russian tanks lost early on were abandoned because they lacked fuel or ammunition. The Ukrainian army certainly did not lose interest in tanks and lobbied hard for them. If there is a need to move firepower over treacherous terrain, then what is required looks very much like a tank. At any rate, it is rarely helpful to look at any system in isolation from the strategic context in which it is being used and the other capabilities available to both sides.

The demonstrable vulnerability of aircraft and tanks provided examples of a regular feature of contemporary warfare – relatively cheap weapons disabling or even destroying very expensive systems. The same point was made by Ukraine's destruction of the cruiser Moskva, flagship of the Russian Black Sea Fleet, on 14 April 2022, using relatively cheap anti-ship missiles fired from shore. Afterwards, the rest of the Russian fleet kept its distance. But there is always a danger in getting too fixated on cost exchange ratios, which look very favourable when air defences are taking out combat aircraft but less so when they are knocking out cheap drones, until account is taken of the costs of repairing facilities that might have been struck by the drones. It is also the case that anti-tank guided weapons have many components that are difficult to replace, while tanks fire simpler shells.

Even when the weapons are individually not too expensive and are relatively straightforward to use, they can soon become a scarce resource. Russia used up many of its precision weapons early in the war and then employed those that remained (and were produced during the war) for attacks on civilian targets where the coordinates were well known, which indicated its priorities. Precision needs good intelligence and the ability to integrate information on the location of enemy forces with the systems by which they could be attacked. It is clear that Ukraine was able to benefit from Western intelligence and also commercial satellites. It was getting harder for Russian forces to hide.

The use of drones has been one of the more innovative aspects of the war. Both sides have used them extensively, although Ukraine was better prepared. The armed Turkish Bayraktar UAVs were effective early in the war until Russia used electronic warfare to stop them. Because of the low altitudes and slow speeds at which they travel, drones can often be shot down. The Ukrainians had a good hit rate against the Iranian Shahed 'kamikaze' drones that were used in attacks on Ukrainian infrastructure, although this has used up a lot of air defence capacity to deal with very cheap weapons. Commercial UAVs became progressively more important to both sides. They were relatively cheap and relatively easy to acquire and adapt, and therefore expendable. The Ukrainians learned to arm them with grenades and use them over short distances against unsuspecting Russian troops, one way of compensating – to a degree – for a lack of artillery shells. The Ukrainians also produced strike drones, able to deliver bombs and missiles over long distances, including into Russian territory.[40] The use of drones indicates the importance of innovation and adaptation during a war. Both sides embraced simple but workable solutions rather than relying on only the most capable, high-performance systems. During the battle of Bakhmut, there could be some 50 drones in the sky above at any time. Their relatively low cost, and therefore dispensability, was just as well. Vulnerability to air defences and electronic warfare meant that few survived more than a couple of flights.

Drones became a vital source of information, another factor making it hard to find sanctuary from enemy fire. The easier it became to observe enemy positions, the more important it became to take advantage of speed. Shashank Joshi of *The Economist* described what might happen with a drone filming a Russian position.

If the operator spots a Russian tank, he can manually mark its location on Kropyva, a Ukrainian-built app, sharing its position with every artillery battery in the area. That system, sometimes dubbed Uber for artillery, has brought engagement times down from tens of minutes to a couple, often the difference between success and failure.

Both sides worked hard to improve their ability to spot enemy positions and bring down fire upon them, which meant that they also worked to disrupt enemy communications. Electronic warfare became increasingly important to both sides. The Russians used powerful jammers to disrupt everything from aircraft to drones to guided munitions en route to their targets. In turn, this led to efforts to target electronic warfare capabilities. They were relatively scarce and emitted powerful signals that rendered them conspicuous. This was one area where the United States could help Ukraine, providing it 'with cuts, or maps, of electromagnetic activity – essentially, the location of jamming and the frequencies used – 32 times a day.'[41]

Access to cheap UAVs is one way armies can compensate for their inability to call in close air support. Russia clearly had an advantage in air power pre-war, yet was unable to make it count. One reason was that surprise was not complete and Ukraine took the opportunity to disperse what resources it could, including aircraft and air defences. Key resources that could not be moved were struck and soon destroyed. Thereafter, Russian pilots appeared inhibited in their ability to manage close air support of ground operations, which can require flying at low altitudes, because of their concerns about Ukrainian air defences, including MANPADS. One possible factor here was that Russian pilots had come from operations in Syria, where they were not bothered by air defences, and so were taken off guard by a better prepared opponent. Even when they were able to mount attacks, they were often surprisingly inaccurate, which probably reflected poor intelligence. There were also coordination problems between aircraft and air defences, which meant that the Russians shot down a number of their own aircraft. The Russians did adapt over time however, including in March 2023 with the introduction of glide bombs (a stand-off weapon with flight controls that allow it to use a gliding flight path onto a target at distance) with which Ukrainian air defences struggled to cope.

The Ukrainian Air Force was not destroyed and managed to keep on flying, though with limited effect. Ukraine's air defences were not put out of action and gradually grew in strength with the delivery of Western systems. The Ukrainian Air Force had trained its pilots to fly their fighters low to avoid radar detection, and they had practised maintaining the aircraft under dispersed and hazardous conditions. Over time, the inventory was depleted, and the lack of modern aircraft and long-range artillery was a source of regular frustration. Some old Soviet aircraft in Eastern European inventories were transferred to Ukraine, and in May the need for a long-range system to take out Russian assets well behind the front lines was addressed by the delivery from the United Kingdom of the Storm Shadow cruise missile.

One duel of particular importance involved the Russian Kinzhal ('Dagger'), an air-launched ballistic missile with supersonic speed, even if it was not quite the 'hypersonic' weapon claimed by Putin. Russia used them sparingly but effectively, and Ukraine appeared to have no answer. In April 2023, Ukraine received two batteries of the Patriot air defence system. On 4 May, a Patriot took down a Kinzhal intended to destroy it, and then on 16 May, six more were brought down during a massive air raid against Kyiv. The Ukrainians never had quite enough air defence – one analogy was of a single duvet trying to cover a king size bed. Yet given the extent of their early vulnerabilities, Ukraine was able to limit the impact of Russia's drones and missiles. Mick Ryan identified it as the development of an integrated air defence system, an impressive achievement involving 'trial, error, and much adaption'.[42]

The most pronounced feature of this war has been the continuing failure of Russian forces to advance much beyond the gains made early in the conflict and not surrendered in the Ukrainian September 2022 offensive. The additional territory taken in the Donbas was achieved slowly and at high cost. As the justification of the 'special military operation' was originally found in the need to protect the people of this region, there was a poignant observation by a local, pro-Russian politician at the end of May 2023. He noted that there was no longer such a 'category as an adult male between 25 and 55 years'. All had been used as 'meat' for assaults.[43] In the process, one of the world's supposedly most formidable armies had been reduced to relying on old equipment and inexperienced and reluctant troops.

Yet still it fought, and while its capacity for offensive breakthroughs declined, it could mount a robust defence, especially in areas where it had been able to construct elaborate fortifications, only approachable through minefields. By this time, the Ukrainian army had been transformed from a largely defensive force, with a popular militia preparing for urban conflict by making Molotov cocktails, into one capable of mounting an offensive with highly capable equipment sourced from the West. But it too had to adapt to the conditions, coming to appreciate the difficulties of advancing rapidly against Russian defences and learning to cope with the special demands of long, grinding struggle.

CHAPTER 3

Total war

A total war philosophy escalates the risks associated with the conflict, especially in the nuclear age, as well as the humanitarian consequences. As all of Ukraine was involved in resisting aggression and occupation, the Russians could claim that everyone was a potential combatant and none deserved immunity. There is, however, a considerable difference between dealing with civilians when they are acting as combatants and deliberately targeting civil society to coerce the government into capitulation.

Such targeting ensures heavy costs – from the numbers killed, maimed, damaged, and bereaved to the ruination of cities and the destruction of infrastructure. The strategic question is whether imposing these costs can be a route to victory, for example by persuading a government that social and economic distress can only be alleviated through capitulation. The strategic impact can also work in the other direction, stiffening the resolve of the population and international supporters to resist aggression.

To assess Russia's strategy of total war, we need to distinguish between what Russian forces did to Ukrainians in the territory they occupied, and their efforts to coerce the Ukrainian government and society. Under the first heading comes actions that reflected a disregard for international humanitarian law, notably tolerating and even encouraging the murder of informants and maltreatment of prisoners, along with rape and looting. Here also comes those actions designed to incorporate Ukraine into Russia, including the 'Russification' of Ukrainian society in terms of language, currency, education, and so on. In this respect, the war was not just inhumane in the ways that all wars tend towards inhumanity. The inhumanity was part of the strategy. The deliberate abduction of children was the aspect that attracted the first indictment from the International Criminal Court (ICC). Russia's readiness to deny the existence of a Ukrainian people and state constituted a genocidal intention, as defined by the 1951 Convention.[44]

BUCHA AND MARIUPOL

There was evidence of a total war philosophy from the start, largely in Russia's carelessness with regard to protecting human life and its breaches of international humanitarian law, with regular strikes against all aspects of civilian life. This often appeared to have a somewhat random quality. At the start of October 2022, the Russians adopted a more deliberate strategy with the targeting of Ukraine's critical infrastructure.

The first damning evidence that Russians were committing war crimes on a routine and systematic basis came as towns around Kyiv were liberated from Russian occupation in early April 2022. Initial indications of atrocities from the town of Bucha were later confirmed by forensic analysis of eyewitness accounts, surveillance cameras, and telephone intercepts to build up a comprehensive picture of when and how they were committed.[45] Lieutenant General Andrei Gurulev, a member of the Duma, who had been directly involved with the separatist militias sponsored by Russia in the Donbas during 2014–15, was recorded on 28 February 2022, just after the invasion, issuing orders to set Ukrainian households on fire. He instructed an invading unit: 'Burn them, damn it, burn them! Once you've thrown them out of there – finish the house, burn it down! Spit at that f---ing humanism!'[46]

After an early attempt to take Bucha was foiled by Ukrainian defenders, causing significant losses, the Russians returned in substantial numbers on 3 March 2022. The small number of Ukrainian soldiers in the town considered putting up a fight but their position was hopeless, so they left. The next day, Russian forces were fully in occupation and were soon checking documents, examining phones, and interrogating individuals. They had lists of people to be interrogated, prepared by the intelligence services. Anybody suspected of being a fighter or assisting Ukrainian troops was tortured and executed, with the aim of neutralising resistance and scaring locals into compliance. Soldiers broke into homes, ostensibly looking for weapons but often stealing whatever they could, including consumer goods, food, and alcohol. One soldier caught on a call home to his mother reported that Russians 'shoot everyone, who gives a f--- who it might be: a child, a woman, an old lady, an old man. Anyone who has weapons gets killed. Absolutely everyone.' The 'cleansing' operations conducted by his tank unit involved seizing weapons, strip-searching suspects, and checking their phones 'to see if there is information or who is against us'. He added: 'If we have to – we will kill.'

Some 400 civilians were killed in Bucha. As *The New York Times* investigation reported:

The victims . . . did not die in the crossfire between Russian and Ukrainian forces, nor were they mistakenly shot in the fog of war . . . Russian troops intentionally killed them, apparently as part of a systematic 'clearing' operation to secure the path to the capital.[47]

The actions were authorised by Lieutenant Colonel Artyom Gorodilov, commanding the 234th paratrooper regiment, part of the 76th Guards Airborne Assault Division, in charge of the Bucha operation and present when civilians were being gunned down. As news of the atrocities came out, to international condemnation, Gorodilov was promoted to Colonel. The crimes in Bucha were not the only ones discovered as Russian forces were pushed back from Kyiv. Some 1,200 bodies were recovered in this region, with reports of deliberate targeting of civilians and escape routes being blocked.

The battle for Mariupol, which began on day one of the war, was the first to demonstrate how much the use of artillery, missiles, and air strikes in support of ground forces seeking to take a defended city could cause massive civilian harm. Apartment blocks and a hospital came under bombardment. The Red Cross described the situation in Mariupol as 'apocalyptic'.[48] By the time Ukrainian resistance was finally overwhelmed in May, some 95 per cent of what had once been a thriving city was destroyed. At times, Russian troops blocked any humanitarian aid from reaching the city. Subsequent battles for key targets in the Donbas – such as Severodonetsk and Bakhmut – left its cities and associated villages devastated. Earlier experiences of the war led Ukraine to arrange for the bulk of the populations to get out before Russian forces reached them.

The successful Ukrainian counter-offensive of early September 2022 in Kherson led to further reminders of egregious Russian behaviour in cities they had controlled. On 15 September, mass graves were found in Izyum (occupied by Russians on 1 April). Ukrainian investigators found 447 bodies in one of the sites, including 414 bodies of civilians (215 men, 194 women, 5 children) and 22 servicemen. Most of the bodies showed signs of violent death and 30 presented traces of torture and summary execution, including ropes around their necks, bound hands, broken limbs, and genital amputation. An investigation found that both Ukrainian civilians and prisoners of war were routinely subject to torture.[49]

A UN-mandated investigative body reporting in March 2023 provided a catalogue of Russian criminality,[50] including attacks on civilians, wilful killings, unlawful confinement, torture, rape, and other sexual violence, as well as unlawful transfers and deportations of children. Attacks on civilian areas and civilian-related infrastructure had been indiscriminate and disproportionate, with no regard for civilian harm and suffering. This pattern of behaviour led ICC prosecutor Karim Khan to begin investigating possible war crimes, crimes against humanity, and genocide early on in the war. On 17 March 2023, the ICC in the Hague issued an arrest warrant for Russian President Vladimir Putin.[51] A warrant was also issued for Maria Lvova-Belova, Russia's Commissioner for Children's Rights. The charges related to the forcible deportation of thousands of Ukrainian children. Unlike other possible areas where charges might be laid, this had the advantage of Russia having made few efforts to hide the program. According to the Ukrainian government, 16,226 children were deported to Russia, of whom 10,513 were located, and 308 returned.[52] The indictment obliged the 123 state parties to the Rome Statute to arrest Putin should he travel to their countries. Whether or not all will comply, at the very least this complicates Putin's travels abroad and how he is received by other states. It also adds to the difficulty of any eventual rapprochement with the West so long as Putin remains in charge.

Prior to October 2022, most Russian missile strikes far behind the front lines were against Ukrainian communications systems and military supplies, although there was a random, opportunistic element too, with strikes also against production facilities and possible housing for troops. In the very early stages of the war, the Russians had some expectation of being able to take advantage of Ukrainian energy assets for their own purposes once the occupation was complete. Special forces were assigned to capture Ukraine's power stations, airfields, and water supplies. The idea that they might be destroyed came only after a full occupation had been ruled out.

The strategy developed in stages. In April 2022, rail traction substations in western Ukraine were targeted to interfere with rail transport. On 8 April, the Kramatorsk railway station was shelled, killing 57 civilians (including seven children) and wounding more than 110. At the time, up to 4,000 civilians, mainly women and children, were awaiting evacuation.

Then the Kremenchuk energy complex, involved in petroleum refining, electricity generation, and oil storage, was attacked three times with missiles. A strike by two Kh-22 missiles against the

Kremenchuk shopping mall on 27 June 2022 killed at least 20 people and injured up to 56.

As noted, the first indication of what might be coming arrived in September 2022 when Russia attacked Ukraine's electricity grid at Kharkiv, leading to a blackout. This followed Ukraine's successful counter-offensive. The most deliberate and systematic set of attacks on civilian-related targets began on 10 October. Although Putin presented them as retaliation for Ukrainian sabotage of the Kerch Bridge, which linked the Russian mainland to Ukraine, a few days earlier, the strikes had been under preparation from the start of the month. They were part of the strategic reappraisal that took place in Moscow after the September setbacks. General Surovikin's strategy was to stabilise the front line so that the Ukrainian army could not advance further, and then try to get the desired result through coercive means. Thus the Kremlin's spokesperson, Dmitri Peskov, justified the strikes by reference to Kyiv's refusal to negotiate on Moscow's terms.[53]

One consequence was a full blackout in Lviv, demonstrating that even Ukrainian cities well away from the fighting could not avoid the effects of the war. Those doing the fighting were less affected, despite Russian suggestions that the strikes were intended to interfere with military operations. The electricity grid was built in the Soviet era, so its design and the location of key facilities were well known to the Russians. The most vulnerable targets were the large transformers that must be in the open for cooling purposes. The most vital took the high voltage electricity from Ukraine's nuclear power stations, of which there are four, with 15 reactors providing more than half of Ukraine's electricity (the one at Zaporizhzhia was under Russian control and kept on the edge of safety through the Russian campaign).[54] The attacks came regularly, but the most severe came on 23 November 2022, when some 70 cruise missiles and 'kamikaze' drones attacked the grid. The system began to switch off automatically. Kyiv lost electricity. Rolling blackouts extended to neighbouring Moldova, connected to Ukraine's grid. The operators struggled to restore power. Eventually, they succeeded.

Thomas Popik, head of the Foundation for Resilient Societies, offered an apocalyptical vision of what these attacks could achieve, indicating possible Russian objectives:

A complete electric grid collapse would likely kill a significant proportion of Ukraine's population. Batteries for communication networks would run down. Government services would cease. Many of

Ukraine's citizens would attempt to evacuate, but when the electrically powered pumps at gas stations stopped functioning, motorists would not be able to refuel. Roads would soon become clogged with stalled vehicles. Some people would strike out on foot, but others would be left behind with dwindling supplies of food and water. Within weeks, famine would probably sweep the country. Without clean water from treatment plants, epidemics could flare.[55]

He envisaged that millions might flee the country, including vital nuclear power workers. After a couple of weeks without power from the grid, the reactors might begin to melt down or fires break out. Similar problems might emerge at hydroelectric facilities, where staff and electricity are needed to manage the dam gates.[56] Commander-in-Chief of the Armed Forces of Ukraine, General Valery Zaluzhny, did not go this far in his interview with *The Economist* in December 2022. But he worried that destruction of the power grid could erode public morale and Ukraine's ability to keep fighting.[57]

Ukraine had to develop a new strategy for dealing with the challenge – including which services to prioritise (hospitals, transport, and social infrastructure) and how to protect key sites. In case the emergency grew in severity, plans were made for mass evacuations. As soon as there was warning of an air raid, the electricity system was powered down, leading to temporary blackouts until the attacks had ceased. Over time, methods were developed to deal with different elements of the attacks. Slow-flying drones were the easiest to shoot down. At first, with only Soviet-era air defence systems, an interception rate of just 20–30 per cent was possible. Once more Western systems arrived,[58] this rose to 75 per cent.[59]

The Ukrainians were resourceful, and they had spare parts stored after past refurbishments of substations. With each challenge, they learned more about their systems and how to keep them operating. After a list of priority items was distributed to Western embassies, help came from the United States and Europe. By March 2023, it was being reported that Ukraine was 'winning the battle'.[60] By April, Ukraine was once again an energy exporter.[61]

To mount these attacks, Russia used around 1,000 missiles and a similar number of drones. They were using more modern but also scarce and expensive systems such as the Kh-22 anti-ship missile (repurposed for attacks on land targets) and Kinzhal air-launched ballistic missiles, based on the Iskander ground-launched missile. With prewar stocks becoming exhausted, they depended on ramping up production of new systems for future strikes. After attacks in February 2023, four weeks passed before the next strikes. The raids involved some of Russia's most expensive items, yet Ukraine survived the coldest winter months and Russia failed to shut Ukraine down. Moscow could also see that a Ukrainian counter-attack was under preparation. By this time, the Russians were shifting priorities away from striking energy facilities to Ukrainian logistics and equipment concentrations, a move that makes perfect operational sense but brought home the strategic waste entailed in the use of scarce resources in a failed attempt to coerce Kyiv into capitulation. As the counter-offensive drew closer, and with more Ukrainian attacks on targets inside Russia, May saw regular, intensive attacks on Kyiv and other civilian areas, but the bulk of the attacking missiles and drones were shot down, with debris the major danger to people. Some of the strikes hit military targets, but the main effect was to add to the stress on civilians and use up air defence systems. Through this period, towns and villages in range of Russian artillery were regularly shelled, and civilian casualties became routine. The constant shelling and mine-laying meant that areas of the country were already covered with unexploded ordnance. The environmental disaster was aggravated early in June as the Ukrainian counter-offensive got underway when, either by accident or design, the Russians managed to blow up the Kakhovka dam in the Kherson region, which was under their control. It was an environmental and humanitarian disaster, with thousands evacuated from low-lying areas either side of the Dnipro River.

July 2023 saw yet another shift in Russian strategy. It pulled out of an arrangement that had enabled Ukraine to export grain, reducing the risk of global food shortages. Moscow would only continue in exchange for substantial sanctions relief.

This was followed by Russian imposition of a formal blockade so that any ships sailing to Ukrainian ports would be assumed to have military purposes, and a series of attacks on the port city of Odesa. Port facilities, grain storage, and the city's cathedral were hit. Ports in the Danube delta, close to Romania, were also struck. Ukrainian air defences struggled to cope. Coupled with the devastation caused by the destruction of the Kakhovka dam and fighting on productive farmland, this threatened Ukraine's long-term economic position.

In response, Ukraine warned that ships using Russia's Black Sea ports would be considered military targets, and reinforced the message by using naval drones to target a Russian military vessel and a tanker.

While Ukraine was unable to contemplate mounting an invasion of Russia or sustaining a regular campaign against Russian infrastructure, it was able to cause anxiety with a few attacks in Russia, largely undertaken by drones in border regions, leading to measures to defend these areas. At first, attacks were occasional and mostly confined to ammunition depots and fuel tanks. Their range expanded over time, even approaching Moscow with a failed attack by a military drone on a gas compression station in February 2023. More successful was a strike using two drones on the Saratov Engels-2 air base, which housed Russia's strategic nuclear bombers. Even more significant was an attack that, according to Ukraine, led to the destruction of a number of missiles being transported through Crimea. An analysis in March 2023 reported at least 27 drone attacks on 'high-value targets in Russia, primarily military bases, airfields, and energy facilities'.[62] Some crashed before reaching their targets and the damage caused was not large.

Because of the way the 'special military operation' had been framed, the fact of these attacks embarrassed Putin. The strikes at the Engels-2 air base alarmed the Kremlin sufficiently for the Russian leadership to get new air defences to protect Moscow, with systems such as the Pantsir-S1 and S-400 appearing on rooftops, including of the Defence and Interior ministries and at a business centre that could provide cover for the Kremlin. On 3 May 2023, there were two attempted drone strikes on the Kremlin, which the Russians claimed, implausibly, to be an assassination attempt on Putin, while Ukrainians denied that it had anything to do with them. More serious were Ukrainian strikes on oil depots in occupied Crimea and on railway lines, in preparation for the coming offensive. Meanwhile, in border areas, some Russian villages had been evacuated and schools moved online. Fortifications had been prepared in border areas, too. The Ukrainians were frustrated by the presumption that they must take continual punishment without being able to retaliate because of American anxieties about the escalatory implications of attacks on Russian territory. One newspaper report cited conversations between Zelensky and his advisers about 'occupying Russian villages to gain leverage over Moscow, bombing a pipeline that transfers Russian oil to Hungary (a NATO member), and privately pining for long-range missiles to hit targets inside Russia's borders'.[63]

In the build-up to the Ukrainian offensive, there were two significant acts of escalation by Ukraine (although they denied participation in both). The first involved a self-styled Russian opposition militia entering the Belgorod Oblast without much difficulty on 22 May and managing to do some damage without great losses before returning. Russia claimed they were Ukrainians and that all were eliminated.

The second came at the end of the month when a significant number of cruise missiles attacked Moscow, most of which were shot down, with only minor damage caused. Putin claimed that this was a Ukrainian response to an attack on military intelligence HQ in Kyiv (for which there was no evidence). This enabled him to allege that Ukraine was following 'a different path – the path of attempts to intimidate Russia, to intimidate Russia's citizens, and of air strikes against residential buildings', as if this was something Russia had eschewed in the past. The cruise missiles were directed at a residential area, although one where the elite lived.[64] In late July, buildings in central Moscow used by security forces were also damaged by drones.

This step was unusual in that it served to warn Russia that its people were not immune to the sort of punishment that Ukrainian civilians were suffering on a regular basis. Other than this, Ukrainian strikes were bold but also limited, and largely geared to military preparations. During the summer 2023 offensive, military sites in Crimea were regularly targeted, especially ammunition dumps. In addition, the Kerch Bridge from Russia to Crimea was put out of action for a second time by maritime drones. Together, all these actions showed how supposed 'red lines' could be crossed in an incremental manner without huge consequences. Russia responded to all provocations with bombastic threats about severe consequences. But, other than nuclear weapons, they had used available methods to punish Ukraine and this had only added to Kyiv's resolve.

THE CYBER DIMENSION

Despite all the effort Russia has put into developing cyber capabilities, its impact has been marginal. This is not for want of effort. The head of the UK's National Cyber Security Centre described the Russian cyber campaign to be 'probably the most sustained and intensive . . . on record'.[65] In the weeks before the war began, a major effort was made to wipe out Ukrainian government networks, deleting data so that systems were unable to function. On 24 February 2022, according to NATO, Russia 'successfully deployed more destructive malware . . . than the rest of the world's cyberpowers combined typically use in a given year'.[66] As of late June 2022, Microsoft claimed to have detected 'eight distinct malware programs – some wipers and some other forms of destructive malware – against 48 different Ukrainian agencies and enterprises'.[67] A significant number of all the destructive malware variants known to exist were used.

The most important attack came one hour before Russian troops crossed the border, when the Viasat satellite communications network was disrupted by Russian military intelligence. According to the Carnegie Endowment's Jon Bateman, this was 'the marquee cyber event of the war so far'.[68] Russian hackers launched a 'targeted denial of service attack [that] made it difficult for many modems to remain online'. They also executed 'a ground-based network intrusion . . . to gain remote access to the trusted management segment' of the network. There they issued 'destructive commands' to 'a large number of residential modems simultaneously'.[69] Some equipment was quickly restored, but Viasat had to ship tens of thousands of modems to replace those that stayed offline. Rescue came in the form of several thousand portable, encrypted ground-communications links to the SpaceX-owned satellite internet constellation Starlink. (Dependence on Starlink came with its own challenges when Elon Musk, its owner, decided he could not allow it to support operations that carried a high risk of escalation by attacking Russian territory).

The attack on Viasat was only one of a number of efforts to jam Ukrainian communications, interfering with links between central command and front-line soldiers. But once the initial offensive faltered, Russia's effort lost focus. Moreover, Russia was struggling with the same problems that had afflicted its conventional military operations: underestimation of Ukrainian defences. There was soon an evident disconnect between the tempo of the Russian offensive and the Ukrainian counters, as well as the management of the sabotage, propaganda, and intelligence-collecting operations conducted by the Russian spy agencies – the FSB and GRU. Despite the talk of hybrid operations, these were not well synchronised.

During 2022, there were 2,100 cyberattacks against Ukrainian organisations, of which some 600 were launched before the start of the war. More than 300 were against the security and defence sectors, more than 400 against civil society (commercial, energy, financial, telecommunications, and software), and another 500 aimed at government groups. From September, when Russia began a systematic campaign against Ukraine's critical infrastructure, using missiles and 'kamikaze' drones, this also became the focus of Russia's cyberstrikes. The attacks included an unsuccessful effort aimed at an electrical substation that would have disrupted power for millions of Ukrainians.

So, despite expectation that cyberattacks would play a major role, the reality was far less impressive. Why was this?

First, it takes time to prepare cyberattacks. It is necessary to get to know the target systems and infiltrate them (increasing the risk of detection). The Viasat attack might have taken a year of preparation. Nor is it easy to switch the same cyberweapons from one target to another.

Second, when cyberweapons are effective, it is not always easy to control their effects. In 2017, the NotPetya virus disabled some 500,000 computers in Ukraine alone but also spread quickly, hitting Russia's state-owned oil company Rosneft and Maersk, the Danish shipping company. At the beginning of the war, Moscow may have had concerns about the political impact of malware spreading beyond the intended target, although it later seemed to be more relaxed about this collateral damage.

Third, cyberwarfare is skilled work. The reported departure of up to ten per cent of IT specialists in Russia during 2022 and the demands of mobilisation will not have helped.

Lastly, and most importantly, having suffered from these attacks since 2014, Ukraine had invested in security and resilience. With the help of governments and international companies, it was able to cope. Cyfirma, a company advising on cybersecurity, explains what was done:

Many crucial services were transferred to data centers outside of the country, beyond the reach of Russian fires. Ukraine's military, contrary to many Russian units, had prepared alternative means of communication. Amazon helped in developing cloud-based backups of essential government data, putting essentially the whole government 'into a box'. Or more precisely suitcase-sized solid-state hard drives, called Snowball Edge units. Critical infrastructure and economic information, more than 10 million gigabytes of data, including information from 27 Ukrainian ministries, have been flown out [of] the country and put into [the] cloud.[70]

NATO provided access to its repository of known malware, Britain provided firewalls and forensic capabilities, the United States pledged large but publicly undisclosed assistance, and the EU's digital governance powerhouse Estonia offered help based on its long-term success in the digitalisation of the economy. Western assistance did not stop with governments and militaries. Amazon and Microsoft alone pledged US$400 million in help, quickly followed by other companies from the industry providing tools and know-how.

It is, of course, always unwise to generalise from one experience, although this was an area in which Russia supposedly excelled. It may well be that a cyber offensive mounted by the United States and its allies would be more effective. As far as we know, Russia has not suffered serious attacks, other than from the hacktivist group Anonymous, which has run a crowd-sourced campaign against Russia. Russian entities have been hacked: printers have printed anti-government messages; hosting servers have attacked Russian websites and services; smart TVs, internet streams, news sites, and TV channels have broadcast banned images and information about the war; and companies that still do business in Russia have been targeted. The impact is unclear, although the Kremlin cannot be pleased, not least because it reveals potential vulnerabilities to more sophisticated attacks in the future.

These cyberattacks have not revealed the potential claimed for them. As noted, they have played a supporting role in the strikes on Ukrainian civil infrastructure, along with missiles and drones. But it has been the missiles and drones that have made it difficult for Ukraine to keep the lights on and people warm. Put crudely, rather than trying to work out how to penetrate a network involved with energy transmission, which might turn out to have effective defences or backup, it is simpler to blast the electricity station.

With direct strikes, the intent is evident and the prospect clear. They are meant to have a coercive effect, and Russia's campaign might have been more successful had the Ukrainians not found ways to improve their defences and cope with the damage. With cyberattacks, coercive value is more limited. They do not normally come with explicit warnings because they tend to be launched anonymously and the perpetrator will be uncertain about whether or not they will succeed.

In addition to its mastery of cyberattacks, another pre-war claim made about Russia was its ability to shape the way people think about the world. Again, there is no doubt Russia believes influencing narratives is a worthwhile endeavour and, as with cyber operations, Russia puts a lot of effort into making it work. There are a variety of audiences – in Russia, the West, and states in the so-called 'Global South'. To keep the Russian public onside, every effort has been made to demonstrate the illegitimacy of the government in Kyiv, the perfidy of the West in supporting Ukraine, and the justice of the Russian cause. With other audiences, the intention may well be to confuse and disorientate as much as persuade.

By and large, the Russian problem is that its narratives are so clearly self-serving.[71] Before the war began, Russian officials mocked US and UK claims that an invasion was imminent. Just before the invasion, Russia claimed a Ukrainian attack against the Donbas was imminent and fabricated an assassination attempt on a DNR official, which was used to justify the invasion. One success was the spread of a false claim that the United States had biolabs in Ukraine, a narrative that was pushed in China, in part because of the links with ongoing disputes about Chinese responsibility for the Covid-19 pandemic. Russia's more successful messaging was to the 'Global South', although this played on established distrust of the West and a dislike of 'double standards'. This was not combined with support for the Russian stance. (Evidence for this lies in UN General Assembly votes, where very few countries backed Russia, though some large countries, notably India and China, abstained.)

Russia's information campaign directed against Ukraine and its supporters can most generously be described as opportunistic and experimental. There has been no consistent narrative, other than the bad things that happened never being Russia's fault. Two examples, relevant to Russian attempts to avoid accusations of war crimes, demonstrate Russia's technique. The first was an attempt to argue that a video taken from a car driving through Bucha featured two actors playing the roles of dead Ukrainians. One allegedly moved their arm while another was seen in the car's mirror sitting up. But it was not hard to show that the first effect was caused by a drop of water or dirt on the car's windshield and the second by the distorting effect of the passenger-side mirror.[72] After the 8 April 2022 attack on the Kramatorsk train station, which killed and injured hundreds, Russian state media pushed the idea that Ukraine was responsible. This included a fake BBC News story that placed the blame on Ukraine. At the heart of this effort was the suggestion that the attack involved a Tochka missile identical to those used by a Ukrainian missile brigade but not by Russians. In fact, there were a number of accounts of the Russians firing this sort of missile.[73] The Russians initially claimed a successful strike against the station until they realised how many innocent civilians they had killed.

To the extent that the Russian narrative had any consistent success, it was in reinforcing Russian support for the war, although this was because of what was said on state-controlled TV as much as

132

social media. Here again, there were problems when particular narratives – such as the inevitable victory of Russian forces, the lack of electricity in Ukraine, and the desperate state of European economies – were undermined by specific events that were hard to deny. On the military side, there were persistent complaints by pro-war bloggers about the inept conduct of the war. These might not have been picked up by a wider audience but were known in elite circles.

Ukraine's information campaigns were more effective. As a Russian speaker, Zelensky was able to make direct appeals to the Russian people. Although during the early days of the war there were anti-war demonstrations in Moscow, Saint Petersburg, and other Russian cities, dissent was soon suppressed. More successful was Zelensky's appeal to Western governments. Because he cut a surprisingly heroic figure and had a natural eloquence (compared with Putin's ponderous speeches, full of obscure references that might be understood in Russia but nowhere else), Zelensky was able to address foreign parliaments directly, where he tailored his message to the audience. The basic point was the same throughout: 'we need more support'. Another important factor was the use of open source intelligence (OSINT) when it came to debunking many Russian claims as well as providing information of value to military operations. The Ukrainian government created an app, Diia, to manage the flow of intelligence coming from volunteers.[74]

Despite the Russian propaganda campaign and hopes that the energy crunch brought about by Russia choking off natural gas supplies would lead West Europeans to abandon Ukraine so that they could stay warm over the winter, public opinion continued to be largely supportive. This made it easier for Western governments to continue to provide military and economic assistance to Ukraine, although their decisions on how best to do this were shaped by the logic of their early commitments, capacity constraints, and concerns about escalation. Even when messaging was based on a strong case and clear evidence (for example, Russian responsibility for atrocities), it could still be tricky to get the narrative right. The most obvious example was when Zelensky's descriptions of the high casualties suffered during the battle for Severodonetsk because of delays in the supply of artillery was taken as a warning of possible defeat. It was still necessary to demonstrate that Ukraine could win, whatever the odds.

NUCLEAR WEAPONS

Nuclear weapons are the ultimate expression of total war. The possibility that Putin might resort to their use has become a regular topic of commentary during the war. However speculative the scenario, or how unclear it remains what Putin might gain by such a move, it has been used by Western commentators in public and governments in private as an argument for restraining Ukraine or at least impressing upon Kyiv why it might be necessary to accept a compromise peace that means conceding territory to the invader.

There is no doubt that Putin regards nuclear use as an option. Russia has a substantial nuclear inventory, with weapons in a variety of shapes and sizes. Also, however foolish nuclear use might be, breaking a taboo that has long surrounded any consideration of their use, those concerned could always note that Putin had already made one reckless gamble in starting the war. But Russia is not short of other means of causing hurt and suffering to Ukraine, and has used those means. As a practical matter, it is not quite clear how straightforward a nuclear option would be. Senior figures might not be inclined to implement orders that came because the president was in a bad temper. Also, Putin reaffirmed with US President Joe Biden in June 2021 the stance taken by

Presidents Gorbachev and Reagan in 1985: 'nuclear war cannot be won and must never be fought'. More significantly, he reaffirmed it again in March 2023 during Xi Jinping's visit to Moscow.

Nonetheless, nuclear weapons have had a major impact on events in Ukraine in a deterrent role. Just before the invasion began, Putin took part in an annual drill involving Russian missiles. Then, when he announced the 'special operation' on 24 February, he remarked that 'whoever tries to hinder us' will face 'consequences that you have never faced in your history'. Three days later, he publicly ordered Defence Minister Shoigu and Chief of the General Staff Gerasimov 'to transfer the army's deterrence forces to a special mode of combat duty'.[75] This did not amount to much in practice; the point was to underline the risks NATO countries would be running if they decided to get directly involved.

Russian figures, including on state media, had made similar threats in 2014 after Russia annexed Crimea. Then Putin stated that other countries 'should understand it's best not to mess with us', adding unnecessarily that 'Russia is one of the leading nuclear powers'. In 2022, as in 2014, Russian media broadcast regular, lurid descriptions of the terrible things Russia would do to any interfering country, neglecting to mention what these countries could do in return. The aim was to present Russia as a country with unlimited power, a will to use it, and little sense of proportion, so that any minor provocation could result in terror raining down on the perpetrator.

Strip away the routine rhetoric and braggadocio, however, and the core aim was still to deter NATO countries from sending their own troops to fight and delivering to Ukraine the means to mount deep strikes against Russian territory. Thus, Russian TV presenter Olga Skabeyeva, who regularly described the conflict as World War III, made specific threats with regard to the potential delivery of the 300km-range Army Tactical Missile System (ATACMS) from the United States to Ukraine. 'Russia has every right to defend itself. That's to say, to strike Poland or the US's Ramstein base in Germany, for example.'[76]

NATO accepted from the start of the conflict that there would be no direct intervention by member states. That was behind the refusal to agree to Kyiv's pleas to set up a no-fly zone to push Russian aircraft from the skies over Ukraine. President Biden was clear that he did not want to give Putin an excuse to escalate. This was one reason why he was reluctant to authorise the transfer of ATACMS. At the same time, the Americans also sought to warn the Russians about the risks associated with nuclear escalation. In a September 2022 interview with CBS, Biden explained that turning to nuclear or other unconventional weapons would 'change the face of war unlike anything since World War II . . . They'll become more of a pariah in the world than they ever have been.' He added that 'the extent of what they do will determine what response would occur'.[77] The dangers were underlined in direct conversations between senior US and Russian officials.

Yet while the nuclear threats were directed against NATO countries rather than Ukraine, Ukraine was the reason Russia was in trouble. Colin Kahl, US Under Secretary of Defense for Policy, said in a statement to *The New York Times* that 'Ukraine's success on the battlefield could cause Russia to feel backed into a corner, and that is something we must remain mindful of.'[78]

But Russia was not being backed into a corner. There was no existential threat to the Russian state, even if one might develop to Putin's personal position. The best way to get out of any corner was to cross the border and go back home. And if Putin wanted to escalate, he had other options. Yet those other options, such as interdicting Western supplies travelling to Ukraine by attacking Poland or Romania, would invoke NATO's Article V, which states that if any NATO ally is attacked, every other member of the alliance will consider it an attack upon them, and come to the aid of their ally. Russian leaders are well aware of this, as they refer to it often. This is how nuclear deterrence worked in the other direction to keep the conflict contained.

If Russia faced calamity in battle, would nuclear weapons be of any value?

Two possible roles were identified: first, to affect the course of the fighting on the ground, and second, to threaten to raise the stakes to terrifying heights and thus persuade the Ukrainians to give up. To a degree, this second role is inherent in the first. Once the nuclear threshold has been passed, then the barriers to further escalation have been reduced. How might this be done? Options ranged from a demonstration shot against a significant but uninhabited site to make the point that a process had been set in motion with an unpredictable end, to direct strikes against Kyiv, with battlefield nuclear use in the middle.

The problem with a demonstration is that the message may be unclear. It would show that Russia was ready to ignore the strong normative prohibition on nuclear use yet still be cautious about making the most of its explosive power. When a similar option was discussed in 1945 prior to the decision to target the city of Hiroshima, one concern was that while this could show that the United States had a new weapon of unprecedented power, and do so without killing large numbers of people, unless the Japanese could see its destructive effects directly it would make no impression on their leadership.

Another issue was whether the bomb would work. It would be embarrassing to encourage the Japanese to watch and then for the spectacle to turn out to be a dud. It is possible that this is a non-trivial consideration for Russia: while missiles are regularly tested, this is not the case with their warheads. As with other weapons brought out of storage, they are not always well maintained and may not work as advertised.

Another decision made in 1945 was not to warn the Japanese of what was coming. Because this would be a lone aircraft, the United States did not want the Japanese to make an effort to shoot it down. As it was, although air raid sirens initially sounded over Hiroshima, the absence of a large raiding force meant that they were turned off, so many people were outside when the bomb exploded. Presumably, Russia would want to keep any attack a surprise to add to the shock value and reduce the risks of it being caught by air defences. Any coercive value would thus have to be extracted after the event, using it as a warning of more to come.

Could this coercive value be combined with real military value? One set of potential targets for limited nuclear strikes are those that have already suffered conventional strikes: critical infrastructure, rather than cities. Alternatively, use could be geared to the battles underway on the ground. Here it is worth noting the issues that surround any attempt to use nuclear weapons as if they are normal weapons of war. In this role, they can be seen as uniquely powerful versions of conventional munitions – bombs, depth charges, shells, and mines, with the added ingredient of radiation. They are best employed against large targets, for example a gathering of troops preparing for an offensive. Ideally, this target would be some distance away from Russian troops. Given the nature of the fighting in Ukraine, this is not at all straightforward. There are rarely massed formations operating in either defence or attack. Units tend to be dispersed.

We have seen no evidence of weapons being moved into position or being prepared for such strikes. US intelligence, which is extraordinarily observant, could be expected to pick up any details (or at least the Russians would need to assume that). No effort has been made to explain to the Russian public why such strikes might be necessary. Putin still insists that this is a limited military operation. As we have seen, Russian figures talk garrulously about scenarios for nuclear use against NATO countries, but not Ukraine. Former Russian president Dmitri Medvedev routinely warned about the terrible retribution that would follow alliance members raising their support to Ukraine, all of which was ignored.

The prospect of nuclear use could engender panic in Ukraine and NATO, but it is hard to imagine that the news would be greeted calmly in Russia. Should the nuclear threshold be crossed, even in a limited way, all bets would be off in terms of a NATO response, which might well include doing exactly those things Putin was trying to deter. Moreover, even if nuclear use did force Ukrainian resistance to crumble, the fundamental political problem would remain: how to pacify a hostile population with a depleted army.

As part of his strategic reappraisal in September 2022, Putin did raise the nuclear issue:

Nuclear blackmail also came into play. We are talking not only about the shelling of the Zaporozhye nuclear power plant, encouraged by the West, which threatens a nuclear catastrophe, but also about the statements of some high-ranking representatives of the leading NATO states about the possibility and admissibility of using weapons of mass destruction, nuclear weapons against Russia. To those who allow themselves such statements about Russia, I want to remind you that our country also has various means of destruction, and in some components more modern than the NATO countries. And if the territorial integrity of our country is threatened, we will certainly use all the means at our disposal to protect Russia and our people. It's not a bluff.

The citizens of Russia can be sure that the territorial integrity of our Motherland, our independence and freedom will be ensured – I emphasize this again – with all the means at our disposal. And those who are trying to blackmail us with nuclear weapons should know that the wind rose can also turn in their direction.[79]

This was still about deterrence. It came at the end of the speech as a warning to the West about further escalation.

Russia worked to ensure that the nuclear issue had high salience even while avoiding authoritative threats to use them other than when Putin's explicit red lines had been crossed. There were missile drills and lurid threats by pundits on state media, and occasionally by other figures such as former president Medvedev. Just after Putin had agreed with Xi in March that nuclear war must never be fought, he announced that 'tactical' nuclear weapons were going to be based in Belarus. There were debates in the West about whether policymakers had taken the dangers too seriously, so that they had not supported Ukraine as energetically as they might have done. NATO countries had been too cautious, it was said, and a realistic risk assessment would have shown that they had more scope to support Ukraine. On the other hand, the incremental nature of the support, so that thresholds were passed gradually rather than suddenly, meant there was never a shock that might have triggered a reckless response.

By the spring of 2023, some of the Russian pundits who had been demanding the most vigorous retribution for various Ukrainian outrages were frustrated that deterrence had failed. Of course, if it had truly failed then NATO countries would have been fighting side-by-side with Ukrainian forces. What had happened was that a number of supposed Russian 'red lines' had been reached and passed, often in small steps, without a big response or just a continuation of punitive measures that had already become routine. This was an example of the limited credibility of nuclear deterrence in the face of incremental developments, each with a marginal impact, even though the cumulative effect might be substantial.

CHAPTER 4

Peace negotiations

Early on in the war, there were a number of efforts to bring it to a negotiated conclusion, but by May 2022 this effort had petered out and thereafter nothing comparable was attempted, not even with a mediator. This was despite the clear international interest in ending the violence and disruption. Economies were taking a big hit and there were concerns not only about the growing rate of death and destruction but also the dangers of the conflict spilling over into something even worse.

It was also despite regular assertions that all wars end with negotiation. Unfortunately, this is not the case. Some wars end with the complete surrender of one party; others fizzle out because neither can sustain the fight, but always with the prospect of blowing up again. Others get as far as ceasefires but no further. Others seem to get further, with some agreement reached, which then proves to be unstable, perhaps because one side is using it to recover and replenish its capabilities after a heavy bout of fighting or because a core issue in dispute has been fudged and the fudge is then exposed.

There are a number of features of this war that make it less than suitable for a major negotiating effort. First, there is no obvious compromise. Either Ukraine is self-governing or is run by Russia; either Ukraine maintains its internationally recognised borders or it has to hand over territory to Russia. There might be extreme circumstances in which Ukraine has little choice but to accept a severe loss of sovereignty, but once it had survived the initial invasion, this became increasingly unlikely. It might struggle to regain all its lost territory, but it will not confirm the loss in any treaty document. Second, the record of agreements between the two – notably the Minsk accords of September 2014 and February 2015 – have left a legacy of mistrust and suspicion. Third, revelations of Russian brutality in Bucha and elsewhere have soured the atmosphere even more.

Lastly, while Ukraine is dependent on Western support and might have been pressured into a deal against its better judgement, Western countries share the negative assessments of Moscow's intentions, and Moscow, at any rate, has given no encouragement to any initiatives. Only after more than a year of conflict, when Russia's war effort was palpably struggling, did China appear as a possible influence on Russian calculations. In general, however, Russia's size and sense of self-importance means that it always assumes it will be the one laying down the conditions. It is therefore difficult to design a settlement that could lead to a moderately stable relationship after one country has been viciously attacked and the other humiliated in battle.

The most natural place to start with any peace initiative is a proposal for a ceasefire. Once agreed, it is possible to move on to a proper peace settlement dealing with the underlying dispute. But the risk of a ceasefire is that there is no subsequent progress: matters are left in a state of suspended animation. The ceasefire in the Korea War agreed in 1953 is often mentioned in this regard as it has yet to lead to a peace treaty. For Ukraine in particular, there is a risk that a ceasefire might turn into a de facto and long-term political settlement, freezing the positions held at the point at which it is implemented, or else turn into no more than a pause before the fighting begins again with refreshed forces.

Direct talks between Ukrainian and Russian teams began soon after the invasion. Russia promised to stop its military campaign 'in a moment', so long as Ukraine acknowledged Crimea as Russian territory, accepted all of Donetsk and Luhansk as independent states, and changed its constitution to pledge neutrality and preclude entry into NATO or the European Union. The original demands for Ukraine's 'demilitarisation' and 'denazification' were never quite withdrawn.

Ukraine saw neutrality as the main area for compromise. On 8 March 2022, when explaining that he was ready for dialogue, Zelensky said:

> I have cooled down regarding this question a long time ago, after we understood that . . . NATO is not prepared to accept Ukraine. The alliance is afraid of controversial things and confrontation with Russia.[80]

He raised the possibility of 'a collective security agreement . . . . with the participation of the world's leading countries', which would provide guarantees for Russia as well as Ukraine. In principle, this had attractions for Putin as it would render Ukraine's membership of NATO unnecessary and would preclude Ukraine from acting as a base for long-range

US weapons. On the other hand, Zelensky would not accept it without some sort of US-backed security guarantee and no demilitarisation. Ukraine had received Russian guarantees before, notably in the 1994 Budapest Memorandum, in return for giving up its nuclear arsenal. The promise then made to respect Ukraine's sovereignty was explicitly repudiated by Moscow on the grounds that the government in Kyiv was illegitimate. The trouble with security guarantees is that they always come with qualifications. In the event of a future crisis, when the guarantees would be most relevant, could there be confidence that future leaders would honour commitments inherited from their predecessors?

On Crimea, Zelensky suggested a compromise that would allow both sides to maintain their positions on to whom the territory truly belonged, while in practice apparently accepting for the moment that it would stay with Russia. On Donetsk and Luhansk, the two enclaves in the Donbas, his language was more elliptical:

> It is important to me how people who want to be part of Ukraine will live there. I am interested in the opinion of those who see themselves as citizens of the Russian Federation. However, we must discuss this issue.[81]

The leaders of the self-declared 'People's Republics' had sought annexation by Russia since 2014. On 21 February 2022, Putin recognised their independence, at a time when these two enclaves amounted to only about a third of the historic boundaries of the oblasts. It was some time since the people of these enclaves had been asked for their views. Moscow would be nervous about the results of free and fair elections under international supervision.

On 10 March, there were high-level meetings between the two foreign ministers – Ukraine's Dmytro Kuleba and Russia's Sergei Lavrov – in Turkey. Soon the Ukrainians sounded relatively optimistic that there might be a breakthrough. In the middle of March, there were even reports of a 15-point peace plan.[82] The core deal was one in which, in return for a ceasefire and full Russian withdrawal, Ukraine would abandon plans to join NATO, although the Ukrainian side of this deal appeared to be more developed than the Russian. The concession from Russia was apparently that neutrality, while precluding membership of NATO and foreign bases, would not require full demilitarisation. Nonetheless, the Ukrainians also wanted security guarantees from other foreign states to prevent attacks on Ukraine. These might not come from NATO but instead from a pool of allies, yet it would still offer the main benefit of being in NATO, if not actual membership.

One problematic aspect of these discussions was that while Russian withdrawal was envisaged, it was not clear whether this would include Donetsk and Luhansk and, most importantly, whether it would be integral to any deal or could be taken as a separate matter for discussion once a ceasefire was in place. One reason for optimism at this time was that Russian forces would be obliged to leave Ukrainian territory soon anyway, because Ukrainian forces were fighting back so effectively. Russia had failed to take any cities, suffering heavy losses in equipment and personnel, and faced unexpectedly severe economic sanctions.

The optimism did not last long. Talks failed to make progress. There were procedural issues still to be addressed even if a deal could be reached on neutrality. Any security guarantees, once agreed, would need to be ratified by the guarantors' parliaments. In addition, Zelensky promised that any deal would be put to a referendum. If agreed, it could take up to a year before Ukraine's constitution could be amended. Also, the big territorial questions could not be put to one side. Once a ceasefire had been agreed, there would be few incentives in Moscow to discuss the return of newly occupied territory. The Russians were also pushing for agreements to restore Crimea's water supply, a Ukrainian pledge not to try to retake the peninsula by force, and the protection of the Russian language in Ukraine. All of this would add to the complexity of any negotiations and the time required for implementation.

Despite the Russian Ministry of Defence's announcement on 25 March 2022 that it would be leaving the area around Kyiv and elsewhere in the north as a 'goodwill gesture' to support the peace talks, as opposed to a concession to military realities, the Ukrainians were now disillusioned with the effort. Discussions continued, with Russia conceding that it was no longer demanding 'denazification' (though only Russia thought Ukraine was 'nazified'), and that it no longer opposed Ukrainian membership of the European Union. Even Russian commentators could not ignore the irony that far from leading to the 'demilitarisation' of Ukraine, the war had led to its intense militarisation.

By mid-May, the talks were effectively over. Lavrov now claimed that the West was using the conflict for its purposes and did not want it to end. More to the point, Ukrainian attitudes were being hardened by Russia's brutal conduct of the war and the evidence of war crimes revealed with the liberation of areas previously occupied by Russian forces near Kyiv. Russia's revised military focus on taking all the Donbas, not just the two enclaves, highlighted the territorial issues.

Whether or not the substantive proposals had merit or could be turned into treaty language, the two large conclusions to be drawn from this early attempt to negotiate a deal were that both sides were influenced by the state of the war, which was not surprising, but also that even an agreed deal could take a long time to implement. An attempt to negotiate a full peace settlement did not offer a quick route to ending the fighting.

PUTIN RAISES THE STAKES

During the early stages of the war, some European countries were looking for a ceasefire, envisaging eventual settlements that addressed the problem of how to accommodate a large, powerful, but badly wounded country such as Russia into the European security order. There were worries that Ukraine's war aims were unrealistic, as it lacked the strength to take back all its territory and so should be prepared to cut its losses. For others, the problem was that Ukraine's ambitions were *too* realistic, for if Ukraine got into a position to free Crimea from Russian rule, might that not lead Putin to use nuclear weapons to prevent total humiliation? By the summer, Western governments were careful to insist that they could not make any deals on behalf of Ukraine. In June 2022, Zelensky persuaded French President Emmanuel Macron, German Chancellor Olaf Scholz, Italian Prime Minister Mario Draghi, and Romanian President Klaus Iohannis to visit Kyiv and see for themselves the costs of the Russian invasion, including the sites of the atrocities at Bucha. The evidence of Russian brutality and lying were important factors in reducing the readiness of NATO countries to push Ukraine into concessions and ramp up Ukrainian capabilities so that it was the Russians who were put under pressure.

Any hope that Ukrainian progress in the war would lead Putin to look for a way out and offer concessions, or even a ceasefire based on current holdings, was dashed by the September 2022 reappraisal. On 30 September, celebrating the annexations of four Ukrainian oblasts, Putin's demands had been raised:

We call on the Kyiv regime to immediately cease fire, all hostilities, the war that it unleashed back in 2014, and return to the negotiating table. We are ready for this, it has been said more than once. But we will not discuss the choice of the people in Donetsk, Luhansk, Zaporizhzhia, and Kherson, it has been made, Russia will not betray it. And today's Kyiv authorities should treat this free will of the people with respect, and nothing else. This is the only way to peace.[83]

Should Kyiv do as he asked and accept the permanent transfer of these provinces, including land that was not even then under Russia's control, it was not clear what it would be getting in return. Putin was presumably still looking for Ukrainian neutrality and the end of sanctions. By this move, Putin boxed himself in, deliberately removing diplomatic options for bringing the bloodshed to an end.

The Ukrainian government's response was that it could not negotiate with Russia so long as Putin remained in power. It now took the view that any discussions on 'post-war coexistence' depended on Russia completely withdrawing troops from all the territory of Ukraine, including the enclaves and Crimea. Zelensky explained:

You don't have time for this diplomacy because they lie. It's not diplomacy. They lie, you know, they want to find 'diplomatic directions' to stop the war. It's lying. Yesterday, they said, 'We are ready, Ukraine is not ready.' And today they attacked us by fifty-four rockets. What? They are crazy.

So, they are ill – I can't understand – on their head. So, what are they speaking about? How can we speak if they attacked us with fifty-four rockets? This day – half of the day. What about are they speaking now? I think they live on another planet. It's not about compromise or no compromise, of course, only victory.[84]

This apparently ruled out negotiations. The Biden administration, working to hold together the coalition supporting Kyiv and address the more sceptical members of the 'Global South', was reportedly nervous about the implications of such a belligerent stance. Zelensky was urged to at least pretend to be interested in a diplomatic solution.[85] In November 2022, in a virtual speech to the G20 meeting in Indonesia, he offered a ten-point plan.[86] Its key feature was that it would require Russia to stop its most egregious breaches of international law and most harmful behaviour, before moving on to outlining a long-term settlement. Restoring Ukraine's territorial integrity was 'not up to negotiations'. Russian troops should withdraw, and hostilities cease. Then 'a Special Tribunal regarding the crime of Russia's aggression against Ukraine and the creation of an international mechanism to compensate for all the damages caused by this war' would need to be established. Ukraine had been attacked because it lacked security guarantees. Zelensky proposed an 'international conference to cement the key elements of the post-war security architecture in the Euro-Atlantic space, including guarantees for Ukraine'. When all measures were implemented, 'a document confirming the end of the war should be signed by the parties'. Somewhat optimistically he added, 'none of the steps above can take long. A month for one step at the most. For some steps, a couple of days are enough.'[87] The speech was a way of emphasising the harm Ukraine had suffered and the illegality and danger of Russian actions. It offered no compromises to Russia.

CHINA'S INITIATIVE

In February 2023, on the first anniversary of the war, Beijing tabled its own plan, urging that:

> . . . all parties should support Russia and Ukraine in working in the same direction and resuming direct dialogue as quickly as possible, so as to gradually deescalate the situation and ultimately reach a comprehensive ceasefire.[88]

The language was critical of the West, warning against 'expanding military blocs' (i.e. NATO), the use of sanctions, and weapons transfers that 'fan the flames', but also referred to international humanitarian law and the need to avoid 'attacking civilians or civilian facilities, protect women, children, and other victims of the conflict', and demanded respect for the UN Charter and 'territorial integrity'. It was limited by its lack of specificity about what all this meant in practice. Russia responded by promising that it was 'open to achieving the goals of the "special military operation" by political and diplomatic means', but with the critical rider, 'so long as the "new territorial realities" in Ukraine were recognised' (i.e. the unilateral annexation of the four oblasts as well as of Crimea).[89] Zelensky was cautious. He demanded a full Russian troop withdrawal (not mentioned in the Chinese plan) but also said he was ready to meet with Xi.[90]

The Chinese were certainly critical of the West but not particularly of Ukraine, with whom they had decent pre-war relations. And if the principles set down in the Chinese paper were applied strictly, then they completely undermined the Russian position. For one thing, the UN Secretary-General had observed that Russia was in fundamental breach of the UN Charter. Around this time, the Russian invasion was condemned 141 to 7 in the General Assembly, with 32 abstaining, including China. As for attacks on civilians and civilian facilities, this was an issue solely for Moscow. The war was being fought among the Ukrainian people, not the Russian.

China's proposal was raised again when Putin and Xi met during the Chinese leader's visit to Russia between 20 and 22 March 2023. Their joint statement contained expressions of belief in the need to respect the UN Charter and international law.[91] No mention was made of the ICC's arrest warrant for Putin for war crimes (with a focus on the abduction of children) with which the week opened.[92] At the same time, the Chinese stopped short of signing up to Russia's justifications. 'The Russian side positively assesses the objective and unbiased position of the Chinese side on the Ukrainian issue.' After chiding NATO for seeking to take advantage of the situation, the statement continued: 'The Chinese side positively assesses the willingness of the Russian side to make efforts to restart the peace talks as soon as possible. Russia welcomes China's readiness to play a positive role in the politico-diplomatic settlement of the Ukrainian crisis.'[93]

On 26 April 2023, Xi and Zelensky spoke on the phone and agreed that Ukraine would send an ambassador to Beijing and discuss China's peace proposals with its envoy.[94] By this means, Xi demonstrated his distance from Putin and set China up to participate in any major reconstruction program in Ukraine.

Among countries unwilling to support Ukraine, either with sanctions or arms, there was a natural desire to instead insist that their interest was in diplomacy. Countries such as Brazil, South Africa, Indonesia, and Saudi Arabia, all significant international players, made visits to Kyiv and Moscow to see what could be done. None made much progress, but their efforts underlined the extent of Putin's intransigence. He treated African interlocutors in a patronising way. When Russia abandoned the Black Sea Grain Initiative in July 2023, creating the prospect of global food shortages and price rises, he misjudged their reaction when offering small amounts of Russian grain free by way of compensation.[95]

When explaining Russia's position, Putin increasingly reverted to the claim that a deal had been available in the spring of 2022, based on neutrality, but that it had been scuppered by Kyiv. This deal, however, demanded that Ukraine recognise 'territorial realities'. Whether Putin would move from this position depended on the degree of military and economic pressure he faced, but also on whether he was persuading countries sympathetic to his attacks on the West for its imperialist and hegemonic attitudes.

At the start of August 2023, Saudi Arabia hosted a two-day conference attended by about 40 countries including Ukraine but not Russia, as well as the United States, India, Brazil, South Africa, the EU, and China. Major themes included territorial integrity and respect for sovereignty, which were closer to Ukraine's position than Russia's. The aim was to establish the basis for a later meeting at heads of state level.[96]

THE PROBLEM WITH PEACE DEALS

A proper peace settlement would need to define the border between the two countries, agree the status of Crimea, possibly offer measures to deal with residents of Ukraine who identify as Russian (presumably far fewer now than before), consider questions of neutrality and security, and address issues of reparations and war crimes. Other parties would need to be involved, as a big issue for Moscow would be getting the many layers of sanctions removed, which would probably only happen gradually as agreements were implemented.

Just stating a possible agenda illustrates the problems facing a conference intended to produce a durable peace. Any settlement capable of being turned into treaty language could not stop the war in short order because nothing could be agreed or even implemented in short order. At best, this would be a two-stage process (and possibly more) requiring separating the fundamental territorial issue – the main driver of the fighting – from all the other consequential issues that might eventually be addressed in a proper peace process. The time has long passed when the two sides could talk directly to each other, so third parties might be important as mediators and then in offering international observers and even peacekeepers.

One role for a mediator is simply to pass messages from one party to another. Another is to come up with creative answers to vexing issues. This requires extensive diplomatic skills but also a prior agreement between the parties, in principle, on some of the fundamentals and a welcome for the mediator's interventions. The third possible role is to strongarm the parties into concessions they would rather not make. The diplomacy around negotiations would be difficult.

One big issue would be the question of what to do about all the sanctions placed on Russia by Western countries. These were first imposed in 2014, and by May 2023 had gone through ten rounds, affecting Russia's trade, finance, and oil and gas revenues, as well as thousands of individuals deemed to be complicit in Russia's war effort. They did not have the hoped-for impact in persuading Putin to abandon the war. Indeed, at first a rise in energy prices boosted the Russian economy. But as prices came down and investment dried up, the strains of sanctions began to show. Unravelling the sanctions regime would not be straightforward, especially if Putin remained in power. Yet if they were not unravelled, it is not clear what Russia could gain in any negotiations in which it would be required to end its aggression and compensate Ukraine for the harm it has caused. One option under consideration was to transfer Russian assets seized under the sanctions regime to Ukraine in part-compensation for the damage suffered.

One of the curiosities of the conflict has been Putin's reluctance to propose a ceasefire, which would freeze the position on the ground. Even though Ukraine would not agree so long as Russia occupied swathes of its territory, there would be propaganda advantages to Moscow. Ukraine might counter by proposing a ceasefire on the condition that Russian forces withdrew to internationally recognised borders and attacks on Ukrainian cities stopped. It would not even be necessary for this to be agreed at a political level. It could be arranged in principle on a military-to-military basis without Putin and Zelensky being directly involved when they are unwilling to talk to each other. Although they would need to approve any concessions, such a device might enable them to reserve their positions on the form a long-term settlement might take.

A disengagement agreement might require that Ukrainian forces would not move into territory being vacated by Russian forces, perhaps to be supervised by an international force of some description (otherwise the Ukrainians would be worried that local people would be left unsafe and uncared for, and that evidence of war crimes would be lost). Such a possibility would only arise if the Russian military had to inform the Kremlin that the position in Ukraine was becoming untenable. Putin remains fearful of the war concluding on anything other than his terms because of the consequential reckoning, as questions would be asked about what had been gained at such enormous cost.

But the more that is included in any apparently straightforward first step, the less likely it is that it will be agreed upon easily or quickly. For example, whatever is decided at this point on Crimea has implications for any future permanent deal. Peace negotiations do not represent an alternative to war. They are best viewed as a continuation of war by other, non-violent means. Without a long-term deal reflected in a treaty, the prospect is one of continued instability, as armies are reconstituted in preparation for further rounds of fighting, even if the conflict has subsided into skirmishing over the short term.

Conclusion

Not a single element in Putin's strategy has worked: not the energy crunch that was supposed to persuade European governments to abandon Ukraine; not the attacks on Ukrainian infrastructure that were supposed to persuade the country to accept whatever fate Russia had in store for it; not the numerous offensives that yielded remarkably little and left the Russian army a shadow of its former self. After the first weeks of war, Russia had a presence in more than a quarter of Ukraine's territory. By August 2023, this was down to 18 per cent, with the prospect of losing more should Ukraine's offensive prosper.

The most important lessons from the Russo-Ukrainian war are about the unwisdom of embarking on major military enterprises on the basis of wishful thinking. On 12 June 2022, I made eight points on the limits of military power.[97]

1. Do not depend on the first military move being decisive. If it is not decisive, you will be fighting a very different war to the one envisaged.

2. A poor performance in the early stages of a war will prolong its length if it does not lead to immediate defeat.

3. It is easier to start wars than to end them.

4. Forces are more determined when defending their own territory than when invading somebody else's.

5. Resistance does not necessarily conclude with the defeat of defending forces but can lead to insurgency. This is why it is always unwise to occupy countries where you will not be welcome.

6. The longer wars go on, the more important non-military considerations (such as national resilience, economic strength, alliances, and partnerships) become to their resolution.

7. During the course of a war, the political objectives for which it is being fought will change so that the prospective gains can justify the actual costs, thereby making the war harder to conclude.

8. The unintended consequences of wars are normally as important, if not more important, than the intended.

I also noted that these rules do not apply in all circumstances. There will always be exceptions. Taken individually, they are perhaps banal but have the advantage of generally being true, and taken together they reinforce each other. By and large, those who start wars tend to end up with much more troublesome and damaging conflicts than anticipated. This happens sufficiently often that any leader tempted to start a war should really be wracked by doubt.

That is why I presumed Putin, who was clearly not risk averse but also, I thought, capable of careful calculation, would have been aware of the dangers of becoming beguiled by the prospect of a quick win over Ukraine. Someone who spoke so often about the war against Nazi Germany would surely be aware of the impact of Hitler's folly in launching Operation Barbarossa. Putin had seen the Soviet Union withdraw from Afghanistan because there seemed to be no satisfactory way to bring its campaign to an end, and then NATO do the same. Why would he make the same mistake in Ukraine?

I had forgotten my ninth rule:

9. As rules 1–8 are self-evident, those political leaders who ignore them and launch a war are apt to achieve surprise simply by being stupid.

After more than two decades in power, Putin's decision-making circle has narrowed. All the voices that might have urged caution are excluded, and his assessments of Russian strength and Ukrainian fragility have been left unchallenged. Putin's blunder confirms the validity of the rules. Like so many before him, he was convinced that this case would be different. The prize of a subjugated Ukraine was just too sweet to be abandoned out of prudence. He is left dealing with a catastrophe, for Russia as well as Ukraine, of his making.

Endnotes

1. Michael Howard, 'Jomini and the Classical Tradition in Military Thought', in *Studies in War and Peace*, (London: Temple Smith, 1970), 21–36.

2. Rupert Smith, *The Utility of Force: The Art of War in the Modern World*, 2nd edn (London: Allen Lane, 2019).

3. John Arquilla and David Ronfeldt, 'Cyberwar is Coming!', *Comparative Strategy* 12.2 (1993): 141–165.

4. Andrei Soldatov and Irina Borogan, 'Russia's Halfway to Hell Strategy: Why Putin has Not Yet Launched a Total War in Ukraine', *Foreign Affairs*, 6 March 2023, https://www.foreignaffairs.com/ukraine/russias-halfway-hell-strategy.

5. Isaac Chotiner, 'Why John Mearsheimer Blames the US for the Crisis in Ukraine', *The New Yorker*, 1 March 2022, https://www.newyorker.com/news/q-and-a/why-john-mearsheimer-blames-the-us-for-the-crisis-in-ukraine.

6. See Lawrence Freedman, *Ukraine and the Art of Strategy*, (New York: Oxford University Press, February 2019).

7. Sarah Rainsford, 'Putin and Peter the Great: Russian Leader Likens Himself to 18th Century Tsar', BBC News, 10 June 2022, https://www.bbc.co.uk/news/world-europe-61767191.

8. Mykhaylo Zabrodskyi, Jack Watling, Oleksandr Danylyuk, and Nick Reynolds, *Preliminary Lessons in Conventional Warfighting from Russia's Invasion of Ukraine: February–July 2022*, (London: Royal United Services Institute, November 2022), https://rusi.org/explore-our-research/publications/special-resources/preliminary-lessons-conventional-warfighting-russias-invasion-ukraine-february-july-2022, p. 26.

9. 'Up to 200 Ukrainian Soldiers are being Killed Every Day by Russian Forces, Zelenskyy Aide Says', CBS News, 10 June 2022, https://www.cbsnews.com/news/ukraine-up-to-200-soldiers-killed-daily-russian-forces-zelenskyy-aide/.

10. Rob Lee and Michael Kofman, 'How the Battle for the Donbas Shaped Ukraine's Success', Foreign Policy Research Institute, Analysis, 23 December 2022, https://www.fpri.org/article/2022/12/how-the-battle-for-the-donbas-shaped-ukraines-success/.

11. Vladimir Putin, News Conference Following Visit to Uzbekistan, President of Russia, 16 September 2022, http://en.kremlin.ru/events/president/news/69366.

12. Carly Olsen, 'Ukraine Says Russia is Retaliating by Hitting Critical Infrastructure, Causing Blackouts', *The New York Times*, 11 September 2022, https://www.nytimes.com/2022/09/12/world/ukraine-power-blackout.html.

13. The Kremlin, Meeting with Members of the Government Coordination Council on the Needs of the Russian Armed Forces', President of Russia, 25 October 2022, http://www.en.kremlin.ru/events/president/news/69676.

14. 'Statements by the Commander of the United Group of Troops (Forces) in the Area of SVO Sergey Surovikin', BMPD Live Journal, 20 October 2022, https://vpk.name/en/643342_statements-by-the-commander-of-the-united-group-of-troops-forces-in-the-area-of-svo-sergey-surovikin.html.

15. Will Vernon and Elsa Maishman, 'Makiivka: Russia Blames Missile Attack on Soldiers' Mobile Phone Use', BBC News, 4 January 2023, https://www.bbc.co.uk/news/world-europe-64159045.

16. Joint Statement – The Tallinn Pledge, Government of the United Kingdom, 19 January 2023, https://www.gov.uk/government/news/joint-statement-the-tallinn-pledge.

17. Ukraine Conflict Updates, Institute for the Study of War, 15 August 2022, https://www.understandingwar.org/backgrounder/ukraine-conflict-updates.

18. Vladimir Putin, Presidential Address to Federal Assembly, President of Russia, 21 February 2023, http://en.kremlin.ru/events/president/news/70565.

19. Isabel Van Brugen, 'Why Russia Wants Bakhmut', *Newsweek*, 8 March 2023, https://www.newsweek.com/why-russia-wants-bakhmut-1786357.

20. Isabelle Khurshudyan, Paul Sonne, and Karen De Young, 'Ukraine Short of Skilled Troops and Munitions as Losses, Pessimism Grow', *The Washington Post*, 13 March 2023,

https://www.washingtonpost.com/world/2023/03/13/ukraine-casualties-pessimism-ammunition-shortage/.

21. Alex Horton, John Hudson, Isabelle Khurshudyan, and Samuel Oakford, 'US Doubts Ukraine Counteroffensive will Yield Big Gains, Leaked Document Says', *The Washington Post*, 10 April 2023, https://www.washingtonpost.com/national-security/2023/04/10/leaked-documents-ukraine-counteroffensive/.

22. 'An Interview with General Valery Zaluzhny, Head of Ukraine's Armed Forces', *The Economist*, 15 December 2022, https://www.economist.com/zaluzhny-transcript.

23. David Axe, 'The Ukrainian Army Lost Bradley Fighting Vehicles and a Leopard 2 Tank Trying and Failing to Breach Russian Defenses in Southern Ukraine', *Forbes*, 9 June 2023, https://www.forbes.com/sites/davidaxe/2023/06/09/the-ukrainian-army-lost-a-leopard-2-tank-and-bradley-fighting-vehicles-trying-and-failing-to-breach-russian-defenses-in-southern-ukraine/?sh=2befo8bb32c9.

24. Daniel Boffey and Pjotr Sauer, 'Putin Denies Zelenskiy's Claims of Counteroffensive Success for Ukraine', *The Guardian*, 13 June 2023, https://www.theguardian.com/world/2023/jun/13/putin-denies-zelenskiys-claims-counteroffensive-success-ukraine-russia.

25. Ben Hall and Roman Olearchyk, 'Military Briefing: Russian "Alligators" Menace Ukraine's Counteroffensive', *Financial Times*, 20 June 2023, https://www.ft.com/content/d8fe8941-3703-433d-ac7a-dab9ba500481.

26. Kieran Corcoran and Mia Jankowicz , 'Russia's Lancet Drone is Hampering Ukraine's Counteroffensive,

Smashing Western Gear and Exposing Poor Air Defenses', *Business Insider*, 14 June 2023, https://www.businessinsider.com/russia-lancet-drone-hampering-ukraine-exposing-poor-air-defenses-2023-6.

27. Yalda Hakim, 'Ukraine War: Zelensky Admits Slow Progress but Says Offensive is Not a Movie', BBC News, 21 June 2023, https://www.bbc.com/news/world-europe-65971790.

28. Isabelle Khurshudyan, 'Ukraine's Top General, Valery Zaluzhny, Wants Shells, Planes and Patience', *The Washington Post*, 30 June 2023, https://www.washingtonpost.com/world/2023/06/30/valery-zaluzhny-ukraine-general-interview/.

29. 'Is Ukraine's Offensive Stalling?', *The Economist*, 25 July 2023, https://www.economist.com/international/2023/07/25/is-ukraines-offensive-stalling.

30. 'Why Ukraine Needs American Cluster Bombs', *The Economist*, 4 July 2023, https://www.economist.com/europe/2023/07/04/why-ukraine-needs-american-cluster-bombs.

31. Franz-Stefan Gady and Michael Kofman, 'Ukraine's Strategy of Attrition', *Survival*, 65:2, 2023, https://www.tandfonline.com/doi/full/10.1080/00396338.2023.2193092.

32. 'Franz-Stefan Gady and Michael Kofman on What Ukraine Must Do to Break through Russian Defences', *The Economist*, 28 July 2023, https://www.economist.com/by-invitation/2023/07/28/franz-stefan-gady-and-michael-kofman-on-what-ukraine-must-do-to-break-through-russian-defences.

33. John Paul Rathbone, 'Russia Has Lost Half Its Combat Capability in Ukraine, Says UK Armed Forces Chief', *Financial Times*, 4 July 2023, https://www.ft.com/content/8cd1c388-6fb9-497b-a8a9-14b6ea21ede2.

34. John Hudson, Robyn Dixon, and David L. Stern, 'Ukraine Launches New Push, Claims Gains against Russians in South', *The Washington Post*, 26 July 2023, https://www.washingtonpost.com/world/2023/07/26/boris-kagarlitsky-arrest-war-ukraine/.

35. Twitter/X, Post by Oleksiy Danilov, 4 July 2023, https://twitter.com/OleksiyDanilov/status/1676116133819170817?s=20.

36. Joshua Yaffa, 'Inside the Wagner Group's Armed Uprising', *The New Yorker,* 31 July 2023, https://www.newyorker.com/magazine/2023/08/07/inside-the-wagner-uprising.

37. Paul Sonne and Anatoly Kurmanaev, 'Russian General Denounces His Bosses as Officers are Fired or Questioned', *The New York Times,* 13 July 2023, https://www.nytimes.com/2023/07/13/world/europe/russia-generals-ukraine-turmoil.html.

38. Twitter/X, Post by UK Ministry of Defence, 6 July 2023, https://twitter.com/DefenceHQ/status/1676828744646795264?s=20.

39. Mick Ryan, 'The Ukrainian Campaign So Far', *Futura Doctrina*, Substack, 15 July 2023, https://mickryan.substack.com/p/the-ukrainian-campaign-so-far.

40. 'Ukraine is Betting on Drones to Strike Deep into Russia', *The Economist*, 20 March 2023, https://www.economist.

com/europe/2023/03/20/ukraine-is-betting-on-drones-to-strike-deep-into-russia?utm_content=article-link-3&etear=nl_today_3&utm_campaign=r.the-economist-today&utm_medium=email.internal-newsletter.np&utm_source=salesforce-marketing-cloud&utm_term=3/20/2023&utm_id=1530234.

41. Shashank Joshi, 'Battlefield Lessons', *The Economist*, Special Report, 8 July 2023, https://www.economist.com/special-report/2023-07-08.

42. Mick Ryan, '500 Days of Learning (Part 1)', *Futura Doctrina*, Substack, 10 July 2023, https://mickryan.substack.com/p/500-days-of-learning-part-1.

43. Кремлёвский Цирк [Kremlin Circus], Telegram, 30 May 2023, https://t.me/KremlCirk/5816.

44. Timothy Snyder, 'Russia Intends to Commit Genocide in Ukraine, Six Ways to Prove It', *European Pravda*, 23 October 2022, https://www.eurointegration.com.ua/eng/articles/2022/10/23/7149219/.

45. Erika Kinetz, Oleksandr Stashevskyi, and Vasilisa Stepanenko, 'How Russian Soldiers Ran a 'Cleansing' Operation in Bucha', Associated Press, 3 November 2022, https://apnews.com/article/bucha-ukraine-war-cleansing-investigation-43e5a9538e9ba68a035756b050 28b8b4/gallery/0fa581cf254a40aebc877ee510876713.

46. 'More Evidence of Russian Atrocities in Ukraine against Civilians Exposed in Intercept – Media', Ukrinform, 2 May 2022, https://www.ukrinform.net/rubric-ato/3473159-more-evidence-of-russian-atrocities-in-ukraine-against-civilians-exposed-in-intercept-media.html.

47. Yousur Al-Hlou et al, 'Caught on Camera, Traced by Phone: The Russian Military Unit that Killed Dozens in Bucha', *The New York Times*, 22 December 2022, https://www.nytimes.com/2022/12/22/video/russia-ukraine-bucha-massacre-takeaways.html.

48. Luke Harding, Julian Borger, and Jon Henley, 'Russian Bombing of Maternity Hospital 'Genocide', Says Zelenskiy', *The Guardian*, 10 March 2002, https://www.theguardian.com/world/2022/mar/09/ukraine-mariupol-civilians-russia-war.

49. Lori Hinnant, Evgeniy Maloletka, and Vasilisa Stepanenko, '10 Torture Sites in 1 Town: Russian Sowed Pain, Fear in Izium', *PBS News Hour*, 2 October 2022, https://www.pbs.org/newshour/world/10-torture-sites-in-1-town-russia-sowed-pain-fear-in-izium.

50. 'War Crimes, Indiscriminate Attacks on Infrastructure, Systematic and Widespread Torture Show Disregard for Civilians Says UN Commission of Inquiry on Ukraine', United Nations Human Rights Office of the High Commissioner, Press Release, 16 March 2023, https://www.ohchr.org/en/press-releases/2023/03/war-crimes-indiscriminate-attacks-infrastructure-systematic-and-widespread; and 'Report of the Independent International Commission of Inquiry on Ukraine', United Nations Human Rights Council, 15 March 2023, https://www.ohchr.org/sites/default/files/documents/hrbodies/hrcouncil/coiukraine/A_HRC_52_62_AUV_EN.pdf.

51. Anthony Deutsch and Toby Sterling, 'ICC Judges Issue Arrest Warrant for Putin over War Crimes in Ukraine', Reuters, 18 March 2023, https://www.reuters.com/world/europe/icc-judges-issue-arrest-warrant-against-putin-over-alleged-war-crimes-2023-03-17/.

52. Ed Vulliamy, '"We Had to Hide Them": How Ukraine's "Kidnapped" Children Led to Vladimir Putin's Arrest Warrant', *The Guardian*, 19 March 2023, https://www.theguardian.com/world/2023/mar/18/how-ukraine-kidnapped-children-led-to-vladimir-putins-arrest-warrant-russia?CMP=Share_iOSApp_Other.

53. 'Kremlin Says it Cannot Imagine Public Negotiations with Kyiv', Reuters, 17 November 2022, https://www.reuters.com/world/europe/kremlin-says-it-cannot-imagine-public-negotiations-with-kyiv-2022-11-17/.

54. Darya Dolzikova and Jack Watling, *Dangerous Targets: Civilian Nuclear Infrastructure and the War in Ukraine*, (London: Royal United Services Institute, 28 April 2023), https://rusi.org/explore-our-research/publications/special-resources/dangerous-targets-civilian-nuclear-infrastructure-and-war-ukraine.

55. Thomas Popik, 'Ukraine's Coming Electricity Crisis: How to Protect the Grid from Russian Attacks', *Foreign Affairs*, 3 February 2023, https://www.foreignaffairs.com/ukraine/ukraine-coming-electricity-crisis-protect-grid-from-russian-attacks.

56. Ibid.

57. 'An Interview with General Valery Zaluzhny, Head of Ukraine's Armed Forces', *The Economist*, 15 December 2022, https://www.economist.com/zaluzhny-transcript.

58. 'Western Air-Defence Systems Help Ukraine Shoot Down More Missiles', *The Economist*, 6 November 2022, https://www.economist.com/europe/2022/11/06/western-air-defence-systems-help-ukraine-shoot-down-more-missiles.

59. Ibid.

60. John Paul Rathbone, '"It's Our Job to Bring Light": How Ukraine's Engineers are Fighting to Maintain the Power Grid', *Financial Times*, 8 January 2023, https://www.ft.com/content/0fe4b288-9fb7-4000-bb57-3e9c57b02d1d.

61. Marita Moloney, 'Ukraine to Export Electricity Again after Months of Russian Attacks', BBC News, 8 April 2023, https://www.bbc.com/news/world-europe-65220003.

62. Janice Kai Chen and Mary Ilyushina, 'Drone Strikes, Sabotage, Shelling: Russia's War on Ukraine Comes to Russia', *The Washington Post*, 20 March 2023, https://www.washingtonpost.com/world/2023/03/21/ukraine-war-russian-soil/.

63. John Hudson and Isabelle Khurshudyan, 'Zelensky, in Private, Plots Bold Attacks inside Russia, Leak Shows', *The Washington Post*, 13 May 2023, https://www.washingtonpost.com/world/2023/05/13/zelensky-ukraine-war-leaked-documents/.

64. Nadeem Shad and Robert Greenall, 'Moscow Drone Attack: Putin Says Ukraine Trying to Frighten Russians', BBC, 30 May 2023, https://www.bbc.co.uk/news/world-europe-65751632.

65. Alexander Martin, 'Russia Waging "Most Sustained and Intensive Cyber Campaign on Record", NCSC CEO Says', *The Record*, 28 September 2022, https://therecord.media/russia-waging-most-sustained-and-intensive-cyber-campaign-on-record-ncsc-ceo-says.

66. Jon Bateman, *Russia's Wartime Cyber Operations in Ukraine: Military Impacts, Influences, and*

Implications, (Washington, DC: Carnegie Endowment for International Peace, 16 December 2022), https://carnegieendowment.org/2022/12/16/russia-s-wartime-cyber-operations-in-ukraine-military-impacts-influences-and-implications-pub-88657.

67. Brad Smith, 'Defending Ukraine: Early Lessons from the Cyber War', Microsoft, 22 June 2022, https://blogs.microsoft.com/on-the-issues/2022/06/22/defending-ukraine-early-lessons-from-the-cyber-war/.

68. Bateman, *Russia's Wartime Cyber Operations in Ukraine*.

69. 'KA-SAT Network Cyber Attack Overview', Viasat, 30 March 2022, https://news.viasat.com/blog/corporate/ka-sat-network-cyber-attack-overview.

70. 'Lessons from Russia's Cyber-War in Ukraine', Cyfirma, undated, https://www.cyfirma.com/outofband/lessons-from-russias-cyber-war-in-ukraine/.

71. See Lawrence Freedman and Heather Williams, *Changing the Narrative: Information Campaigns, Strategy and Crisis Escalation in the Digital Age*, (London: International Institute for Strategic Studies, 2023).

72. Bill McCarthy, 'Russia Pushes False Crisis Actor Claims about Video from Bucha, Ukraine', *Politifact*, 4 April 2022, https://www.politifact.com/factchecks/2022/apr/04/russian-ministry-defense/russia-pushes-false-crisis-actor-claims-about-vide/.

73. Samantha Putterman, 'No Evidence that Ukraine Attacked a Train Station in One of its Cities', *Politifact*, 18 April 2022, https://www.politifact.com/factchecks/2022/apr/18/facebook-posts/no-evidence-ukraine-attacked-train-station-one-its/.

74. Peter W. Singer, 'One Year In: What are the Lessons from Ukraine for the Future of War?', *Defense One*, 22 February 2023, https://www.defenseone.com/ideas/2023/02/what-ukraine-has-changed-about-war/383216/.

75. Matthew Luxmoore, 'Putin Puts Nuclear Forces in a "Special Mode of Combat Duty"', *The Wall Street Journal*, 28 February 2022, https://www.wsj.com/livecoverage/russia-ukraine-latest-news-2022-02-26/card/putin-puts-nuclear-forces-in-a-special-mode-of-combat-duty--WKMRkTauWFNnWy26hZar.

76. Twitter/X, Post by Francis Scarr, 19 September 2022, https://twitter.com/francis_scarr/status/1571821303253946368.

77. 'President Biden Warns Vladimir Putin Not to Use Nuclear Weapons: "Don't. Don't. Don't."', CBS News, 16 September 2022, https://www.cbsnews.com/news/president-joe-biden-vladimir-putin-60-minutes-2022-09-16/.

78. David Sanger, Anton Troianovski, Julian Barnes, and Eric Schmitt, 'Ukraine Wants the US to Send More Powerful Weapons. Biden is Not So Sure', *The New York Times*, 17 September 2022, https://www.nytimes.com/2022/09/17/us/politics/ukraine-biden-weapons.html.

79. Vladimir Putin, '"Will Make Use of All Weapon Systems Available": What Putin Said while Ordering Partial Mobilisation', *The Wire*, 21 September, 2022, https://thewire.in/world/full-text-vladimir-putin-speech-nuclear-russia-ukrain-nato.

80. Christiane Amanpour, Tweet of statement by Volodymyr Zelensky, Twitter, 11 March 2022, https://twitter.com/amanpour/status/1501925573769273348.

81. Volodymyr Zelensky, 'Ukraine Must Have a Collective Security Agreement with all its Neighbors with the Participation of the World's Leading Powers – President', President of Ukraine, 8 March 2022, https://www.president.gov.ua/en/news/ukrayina-povinna-mati-kolektivnij-dogovir-bezpeki-zi-vsima-s-73433.

82. Max Seddon, Roman Olearchyk, Arash Massoudi, and Neri Zilber, 'Ukraine and Russia Explore Neutrality Plan in Peace Talks', *Financial Times*, 17 March 2022, https://www.ft.com/content/7b341e46-d375-4817-be67-802b7fa77ef1.

83. 'Extracts from Putin's Speech at Annexation Ceremony', Reuters, 1 October 2022, https://www.reuters.com/world/extracts-putins-speech-annexation-ceremony-2022-09-30/.

84. Brandon Gage, 'Zelenskyy Says Russia's Peace Calls are "Crazy"', *Salon*, 3 November 2022, https://www.salon.com/2022/11/03/zelenskyy-says-peace-calls-are-crazy_partner/.

85. Missy Ryan, John Hudson, and Paul Sonne, 'US Privately Asks Ukraine to Show it's Open to Negotiate with Russia', *The Washington Post*, 5 November 2022, https://www.washingtonpost.com/national-security/2022/11/05/ukraine-russia-peace-negotiations/.

86. Volodymyr Zelensky, 'Ukraine has Always been a Leader in Peacemaking Efforts; if Russia Wants to End this War, Let it Prove it with Actions', Speech

by the President of Ukraine at the G20 Summit, President of Ukraine, 15 November 2022, https://www.president.gov.ua/en/news/ukrayina-zavzhdi-bula-liderom-mirotvorchih-zusil-yaksho-rosi-79141?fbclid=IwAR0r3lTXwo4wl38e8G1KS4rlv_7luNK0RIM-qPpk5GYBkz37VW8ZSmzhG0s.

87. Ibid.

88. 'China's Position on the Political Settlement of the Ukraine Crisis', Ministry of Foreign Affairs of the People's Republic of China, 24 February 2023, https://www.fmprc.gov.cn/mfa_eng/zxxx_662805/202302/t20230224_11030713.html.

89. 'Russia Welcomes China Peace Plan, Says it is Open to Talks', Reuters, 25 February 2023, https://www.reuters.com/world/europe/russia-welcomes-china-peace-plan-says-it-is-open-talks-2023-02-24/.

90. 'Ukraine Welcomes Some Chinese Ceasefire "Thoughts", Insists on Russian Withdrawal', Reuters, 25 February 2023, https://www.reuters.com/world/ukraine-says-its-open-some-parts-china-ceasefire-proposal-2023-02-24/.

91. 'Joint Statement by the Russian Federation and the People's Republic of China on Deepening Comprehensive Partnership and Strategic Cooperation, Entering a New Era', President of Russia, 21 March 2023, http://kremlin.ru/supplement/5920.

92. Deutsch and Sterling, 'ICC Judges Issue Arrest Warrant for Putin Over War Crimes in Ukraine'.

93. 'What Russia–Chinese Joint Statement Says about Ukraine', Reuters, 22 March 2023, https://www.reuters.

com/world/what-russia-chinese-joint-statement-says-about-ukraine-2023-03-21/.

94. 'At Last, Xi Jinping Calls Volodymyr Zelensky', *The Economist*, 26 April 2023, https://www.economist.com/china/2023/04/26/at-last-xi-jinping-calls-volodymyr-zelensky.

95. Mark Trevelyan and Kevin Liffey, 'African Leaders Tell Putin: "We Have a Right to Call for Peace"', Reuters, 29 July 2023, https://www.reuters.com/world/putin-tells-african-leaders-moscow-is-studying-their-ukraine-proposal-2023-07-28/.

96. Lisa O'Carroll, 'China "Backs Further Ukraine Peace Talks" after Saudi Arabia Summit', *The Guardian*, 6 August 2023, https://www.theguardian.com/world/2023/aug/06/china-backs-further-ukraine-peace-talks-saudi-arabia-summit.

97. Lawrence Freedman, 'Spirits of the Past', *Comment is Freed*, 12 June 2022, https://samf.substack.com/p/spirits-of-the-past.

Acknowledgements

The author is grateful to Sam Roggeveen for persuading me to write this book and seeing it through to fruition, and Clare Caldwell for her editing. I am also grateful to the two anonymous reviewers for their excellent and constructive comments. I should note that some sections of the book draw on material that originally appeared in my substack *Comment is Freed* (https://samf.substack.com/).

Lowy Institute Penguin Specials

PENGUIN
SPECIALS

RISE OF THE EXTREME RIGHT

Lydia Khalil

A LOWY INSTITUTE PAPER

ASIO says right-wing extremism now makes up half its case load, and that it anticipates a terrorist attack on Australian soil within the year. There has been a 250 per cent increase in right-wing terrorism globally. So what exactly is right-wing extremism and how is its potential for violence growing? Why is it a global problem? How does it threaten democracy and what should we do about it? *Rise of the Extreme Right* answers these questions while situating Australia within the global threat landscape.

MORRISON'S MISSION

Paul Kelly

A LOWY INSTITUTE PAPER

When he became Prime Minister in 2018, Scott Morrison was a foreign policy amateur confronted by unprecedented challenges: an assertive Beijing and a looming rivalry between the two biggest economies in world history, the United States and China. Morrison plunged into foreign and security policy by making highly contentious changes that will be felt for decades, not least the historic decision to build nuclear-powered submarines.

Featuring interviews with Morrison and members of his cabinet, this book tells the story of the Prime Minister's foreign policy convictions and calculations, and what drove his attitudes towards China, America and the Indo-Pacific.

PENGUIN
SPECIALS

RECONSTRUCTION

John Edwards

A LOWY INSTITUTE PAPER

What kind of future do Australians have?

Until the coronavirus pandemic, nearly two-thirds of Australians had never experienced an economic slump in their working lives. Indeed, nearly half were not yet born when the Australian economy last tipped into recession. Creating a path for Australia through these difficult times requires a careful assessment of where we have come from, where we are, and where we are going.

This Paper, by one of Australia's leading economic voices, examines the fractured state of the global economy and financial system, the ailing US economy and its epic contest with China, the global economic order, and what it all means for us.

PENGUIN
SPECIALS

MAN OF CONTRADICTIONS

Ben Bland

A LOWY INSTITUTE PAPER

From a riverside shack to the presidential palace, Joko Widodo surged to the top of Indonesian politics on a wave of hope for change. However, six years into his presidency, the former furniture maker is struggling to deliver the reforms that Indonesia desperately needs. Despite promising to build Indonesia into an Asian powerhouse, Jokowi, as he is known, has faltered in the face of crises, from COVID-19 to an Islamist mass movement.

Man of Contradictions, the first English-language biography of Jokowi, argues that the president embodies the fundamental contradictions of modern Indonesia. He is caught between democracy and authoritarianism, openness and protectionism, Islam and pluralism. Jokowi's incredible story shows what is possible in Indonesia — and it also shows the limits.

OUR VERY OWN BREXIT

Sam Roggeveen

A LOWY INSTITUTE PAPER

Could Australia have a Brexit moment?

There is a rarely spoken truth at the heart of Australian politics:
it is dominated by two parties that voters no longer care about.

Around the democratic West, the public is drifting away from
major parties, and politics is becoming hollow. In Europe,
populists have been the beneficiaries. In Britain, the result was
Brexit.

Australian politics is hollow, too. One of our declining parties
could, in desperation, exploit an issue that ties Australia to Asia
and which will determine our future security: immigration.